"If you're looking for a no-frills A–Z book with ju[...] your checkbook, don't buy this book. However, i[...] help you along the path to financial understanding, peace of mind, and service to God with your finances, then this is the book for you. Matt Bell is a prodigal who understands the grace of God, the principles of God, and how to communicate them in a practical, fun, and relational way. Matt helps you find God's plan for your life and your money, and this book should be your first investment!"

—STEVE MOORE, Crown Financial Ministries

"Matt provides a vision for using money in a way that brings freedom and joy, along with the practical steps for getting there."

—NANCY ORTBERG, founding partner, Teamworx2

"You hold in your hands a book of joy! Like two old friends, money and joy meet up again when you let Matt Bell free you to use money as an expression of the generous heart God has already given you."

—DR. BRUCE McNICOL, president, Leadership Catalyst;
author of *TrueFaced*, *Bo's Café*, and *The Ascent of a Leader*

"Matt writes from the heart with passion, conviction, and credibility. His message is not about the obligation of biblical money management but about the adventure and joy."

—DICK TOWNER, executive director,
Good $ense Stewardship Movement

"This book provides a pathway toward financial freedom and joy. Matt Bell grounds his work in scriptural truth and weaves his own journey with money throughout each chapter. I can't imagine a more relevant issue in our time than the challenge to manage our resources so that God is honored, we are at peace, and we experience the fulfillment of contributing to the needs of our broken world."

—NANCY BEACH, executive vice president of programming and production,
Willow Creek Association; author of *An Hour on Sunday*

"There are books, magazines, movies, and even songs about money, yet money remains something of a mystery to many people. Matt demystifies the subject by showing how to connect our use of money with all that makes life meaningful."

—JACKSON CRUM, senior pastor, Park Community Church, Chicago

Matt Bell

The Proven Path
to Uncommon
Financial Success

MONEY

PURPOSE

JOY

NavPress is the publishing ministry of The Navigators, an international Christian organization and leader in personal spiritual development. NavPress is committed to helping people grow spiritually and enjoy lives of meaning and hope through personal and group resources that are biblically rooted, culturally relevant, and highly practical.

For a free catalog go to www.NavPress.com
or call 1.800.366.7788 in the United States or 1.800.839.4769 in Canada.

Library of Congress Cataloging-in-Publication Data

Bell, Matt, 1960-
  Money, purpose, joy : the proven path to uncommon financial success /
Matt Bell.
    p. cm.
  Includes bibliographical references.
  ISBN 978-1-60006-279-7
  1. Finance, Personal. 2. Finance, Personal--Religious
aspects--Christianity. I. Title.
  HG179.B373 2008
  332.024--dc22
                          2008011693

Printed in the United States of America

1 2 3 4 5 6 7 8 / 12 11 10 09 08

For Jude

Living the adventure of life with you is a daily reminder
of how much God loves me.

CONTENTS

Ah, but a man's reach should exceed his grasp,
or what's a heaven for?

— ROBERT BROWNING, *ANDREA DEL SARTO*

Part One

Where We Are

A person who strays from home is like a bird that strays
from its nest.

— PROVERBS 27:8 (NLT)

The younger son gathered all he had and took a journey
into a far country.

— LUKE 15:13 (ESV)

Chapter 1

WANDERING FROM HOME

After one of my first financial workshops, in which I shared part of my journey, a participant approached me with a question and casually referred to my "prodigal son story." Until then, I hadn't made the connection. That night, as I reread the biblical story of the prodigal son, I was amazed at how similar it was to my own story.

> There was a man who had two sons. The younger one said to his father, "Father, give me my share of the estate." So he divided his property between them.
>
> Not long after that, the younger son got together all he had, set off for a distant country and there squandered his wealth in wild living.[1]

Three years after graduating from college, I received an inheritance of $60,000 from an uncle. At the time, I was earning around $25,000 a year working as a freelance radio journalist. When I received the unexpected check for more than twice my annual income, I felt as if I'd won the lottery. I saw the inheritance as an incredible, once-in-a-lifetime opportunity.

I decided to use the windfall to create my dream job. I wanted to be one of those rare people who actually looked forward to Mondays.

I took a quick inventory of the things I most enjoyed; golf and travel topped the list. Then I stirred in my profession of journalism and came up with the idea of writing a newsletter for people who take golf vacations.

What could be better than trekking around the world, traveling from resort to resort, reporting on the best places to play? I bought some desktop publishing software, took out an ad for the newsletter in a golf magazine, booked my first trip, and *Links Review* was born.

Once a month I traveled to a beautiful vacation spot to review, photograph, and, of course, play the best golf courses in the area. I went to Puerto Rico; southern Spain and Portugal; Orlando, Florida; Pinehurst, North Carolina; and the Pebble Beach/Carmel area of California. Stories about my newsletter appeared in publications such as *Golf Magazine* and the *Chicago Sun-Times*. When I was home, I used my newfound wealth to enjoy the better restaurants Chicago has to offer and to buy clothing from the city's higher-end shops. I looked the part of a successful, young entrepreneur. Never mind that my newsletter had few paid subscribers. That seemed like a minor detail since I had what felt like an endless supply of money in the bank. So I kept traveling, writing, and enjoying myself. The entrepreneurial life was everything I dreamed it would be—except profitable.

> After he had spent everything, there was a severe famine in that whole country, and he began to be in need. So he went and hired himself out to a citizen of that country, who sent him to his fields to feed pigs. He longed to fill his stomach with the pods that the pigs were eating, but no one gave him anything.[2]

I soon discovered that when you spend a lot more than you make every month, even when you start with a healthy cash cushion, it doesn't take long to get in a jam. Two years after receiving the inheritance, I was in financial trouble. Deep trouble. Not only had I squandered the $60,000 but I'd spent so much more—$20,000 more—that I could not make the minimum payments on my credit cards while still paying for food and rent.

> When he came to his senses, he said, "How many of my father's hired men have food to spare, and here I am starving to death!

I will set out and go back to my father and say to him: Father, I have sinned against heaven and against you. I am no longer worthy to be called your son; make me like one of your hired men." So he got up and went to his father.[3]

As I began realizing the depth of my financial problems, my parents sensed that all was not right and asked me to come see them for a little chat.

While he was still a long way off, his father saw him and was filled with compassion for him; he ran to his son, threw his arms around him and kissed him.

The son said to him, "Father, I have sinned against heaven and against you. I am no longer worthy to be called your son."

But the father said to his servants, "Quick! Bring the best robe and put it on him. Put a ring on his finger and sandals on his feet. Bring the fattened calf and kill it. Let's have a feast and celebrate. For this son of mine was dead and is alive again; he was lost and is found." So they began to celebrate.[4]

My parents didn't hold a celebration in my honor, but they graciously invited me to move in with them in order to help me turn my situation around. I will always be grateful for their support. I don't know what I would have done otherwise. However, to go from the good life I was living to residing in my parents' basement in the small town where I grew up? That was brutal.

For two months of what would become a six-month stay, I was depressed. I looked forward to the nighttime, when I could close my eyes and sleep. I wanted to forget about the way I had mismanaged my uncle's money and wasted the chance to live my dream. I dreaded the coming of each new day, when I had to face the reality of my situation. Over and over I reminded myself of the obvious: I didn't know the first thing about managing money. Anyone who could take $60,000 and turn it into negative $20,000 was not exactly a money-management genius.

A New Beginning

But hitting bottom became a catalyst for some positive changes in my life. First, I became motivated to learn how to manage money well. I devoured every personal-finance book and magazine I could get my hands on, and I've been studying the topic ever since.

Second, I started thinking about the big questions of life: *What's my purpose? Where do I go from here?* Right about then, I received a phone call that marked the beginning of a life-changing spiritual journey.

Wayne and I had been in the same broadcast journalism program in college, and we had worked together at a public radio station while we were students. I graduated a year ahead of him and moved out of state for a job, and we fell out of touch. When Wayne heard that financial problems had led me to move back home with my parents, which wasn't far from where he lived, he gave me a call. Unknown to me, during his last year in college, Wayne's faith had become the center of his life.

I grew up in a family that rarely went to church. My father was a nonpracticing Jew, my mother a nonpracticing Catholic. Even though my father had told my mother he would not marry her if she insisted on raising their children as Catholics, she somehow passed down to me her basic beliefs. I grew up believing that Jesus is the Son of God and in heaven. But that's about as far as it went; those beliefs had little influence on how I lived my life.

When Wayne and I got together to talk, I'll never forget his stark conclusion about the mess I'd made of my finances: "The more you've leaned on your own understanding, Matt, the more things haven't worked out so well."[5] He also offered a few hopeful comments, such as, "God has a plan for your life."[6] As I thought about it, I had to agree with his first statement, and his second one intrigued me. I had no idea what might be next, so the suggestion that someone *did* know got my attention. My respect for Wayne, his passion for his convictions, my circumstances, and the notion that there may be some plan for my life made me want to learn more about matters of faith. While maintaining the skepticism of a journalist, I began reading the Bible. I even started going to church.

Four months after moving in with my parents, I went back to work as a freelance radio reporter. A couple of months later, I was back in Chicago, living in a studio apartment. Committed to getting out from under my pile of debt, I was taking on any story assignment I could get—working nights, weekends, whatever it took to earn as much money as possible. I also had begun dating someone I met at church.

One night, after an upsetting argument that put the future of the relationship in doubt, I found myself in the quiet of my tiny apartment, feeling very broken. It was all too similar to the feeling I had when my golf newsletter was going under. Wayne's observations echoed in my head: *The more you've leaned on your own understanding, Matt, the more things haven't worked out so well* and *God has a plan for your life*. I realized that I was still working *my* plan and, once again, it wasn't working out so well. I bowed my head and prayed a simple prayer: *God, if you really do exist, I'd like to know you. If you really do have a plan for my life, I'd sure like to know what it is. I'm sorry for the many ways I must have disappointed you and for making myself the focus of my life. From this point forward, my life is in your hands. Do with it what you will. Amen.*

Two Journeys Become One

I didn't see any lightning bolts, the clouds didn't part, and no weeping angels appeared. But after committing my life to Christ, I began to study the Bible more closely. The more I read it, the more I realized that it has a lot to say about money. Much of what I was learning about a life of faith was directly relevant to how I managed my finances. What I'd thought were two separate journeys—my financial journey and my spiritual journey—were tightly bound together.

One of my biggest aha moments was when I realized that many of the cultural messages about managing money are completely wrong. Instead of moving us toward greater success and happiness, they push us in the opposite direction. As I began helping others with their finances, I started seeing that our acceptance of the common beliefs about money management has turned many of us into prodigal sons and daughters, leading us away from home—*home* being a metaphor for all that truly matters and makes life meaningful.

Many financial teachers who want to help people move in a better direction with their money share a common recommendation—namely, to stop stretching so far. It's a reasonable-sounding idea, logical even, what with the savings rate and debt levels where they are. But it, too, is wrong. The real solution is that we need to stop settling for so little.

Turning toward home, toward uncommon financial success, requires that we set our sights higher, that we become clear about what truly matters and who we were made to be. It involves looking beyond the many cultural distractions that seem intent on pulling us off course, and keeping our eyes fixed and our money focused on that which gives our lives meaning, purpose, and joy. It involves refusing to settle for anything less. When we turn toward home, our use of money becomes a powerful expression of who we are and what we're about.

I wrote this book to help you make that turn and stay on the financial path toward all that's most important to you. The rest of part 1 will help you see how far you may have wandered from home in your use of money and why; part 2 will help you clarify what really matters so that you can orient your financial choices around those priorities; in parts 3 and 4 you'll learn specific steps that'll help you use money in a way that expresses those priorities.

At the end of each chapter, you'll find a short summary of the chapter's key points, some action steps, and a verse of Scripture related to the chapter for further reflection. Throughout the book, you'll also find several forms to help you act on what you're learning. If you are using the personal workbook, it contains full-sized versions of the forms along with additional forms and other tools that will help you go further with the practical applications. In addition to the workbook, a companion study guide is available for group or individual use. It will help you dig deeper into matters of the heart as they pertain to money and dive more deeply into God's Word.

Lasting behavioral changes begin with internal changes—changes in how you think and what you believe—so that's where we're going to start. For a financial book, this is an uncommon approach. But I assume you're interested in uncommon results. Not just the appearance of success or short-term success, but true and lasting success. Not just financial peace, but financial joy.

The process you are about to learn has enabled many of the people I've worked with over the past eighteen years to achieve their financial goals, such as getting and staying out of debt or building savings. For others, it has meant learning how to use money in a way that brings greater meaning and fulfillment. For most, it has meant some of both.

Much of what follows will feel countercultural because it contradicts many of the messages that surround us — messages that more often than not hurt our finances and hinder our happiness. But it won't feel counterintuitive because this book is about getting reacquainted with some of your deepest desires and allowing them to guide you toward home, toward the most effective, joyful use of money.

Chapter 2

FINANCIALLY
TRUE OR FALSE?

All the world's a stage.

— WILLIAM SHAKESPEARE

All the world is not, of course, a stage, but the crucial ways in which it isn't are not easy to specify.

— ERVING GOFFMAN

It took me four and a half years to pay off my credit card debts and another three years to pay off my car. During that time, I began doing volunteer work in which I counseled people about their finances one on one. Before long, I was teaching workshops about money management. The joy of helping others enabled me to see a larger purpose for what I went through, and it changed how I viewed my experience. At first I thought my story was unique. Surely I must be in the minority; most people don't struggle with money. Just look around. People are driving nice cars, living in nice homes. Most folks look as though they're doing just fine.

I soon found out just how wrong I was. As I worked with more and more people in seminars and individual coaching sessions, I realized that underneath the surface of their lives, many folks carry a great deal of financial stress, confusion, fear, and disappointment—not to mention a lot of debt and minimal savings. Since you are reading this book, it's likely that you can relate.

Maybe you find it difficult to save. If so, you have lots of company. The average household's savings rate is now approximately 0 percent of disposable income.[1]

Maybe your debt load feels a bit heavy. Here again, you're not alone. Nearly 60 percent of households with credit cards carry a balance from month to month.[2]

How often do you worry about money? More than 70 percent of adults say they do so either "often" (35 percent) or "sometimes" (37 percent).[3]

Do you ever argue about money with the people you're closest to? Therapists say money is one of the most common causes of conflict among married couples.

Finally, how happy are you? One trend over the past thirty years that I find surprising is that happiness has not grown. It doesn't seem to matter that many more people have achieved the American dream of home ownership over that time, acquired all manner of electronic gear (from computers to cell phones to big-screen televisions), and taken international vacations. The percentage of people who feel "very happy" has remained remarkably stagnant.[4]

There is a wealth of financial information and teaching available today, telling us exactly where to save and what to invest in, which professions pay the most and which retirement towns cost the least, how to buy a house and settle an estate, how to get the best deals on cars or a Caribbean cruise, and, most of all, how to get rich. Still, getting the money thing right is not so easy for most of us.

Clearly, we need more than how-to information if we are going to make the most of our money. It's not that how-to advice is unimportant; it's just that focusing too early on the how-to steps is like trying to find our way out of a forest without any sense of where we are. So in this part of the book, we are going to clarify where we are and how we got here.

Our True Desires and Their Imposters

During our second year of marriage, my wife, Jude, and I took a trip to Italy. In Florence, we went to see Michelangelo's famous sculpture *David*.

We learned that when Michelangelo began working on a sculpture, he often felt as though he were revealing the shape that was already inside. Where most people saw just a chunk of marble, Michelangelo saw something beautiful.

Similarly, within each of us is what I call our *true desires*—powerful, heartfelt longings for that which makes life worth living. I call them *true* desires because the objects of these desires provide us with the rich fulfillment we all want; they are the elements of life that really matter, that give our lives meaning and joy. Our true desires are the road signs that point the way home, guiding us toward the most successful, satisfying use of money.

When we're not clear about what really matters in life, we leave ourselves open to the many cultural suggestions as to what will make us happy, which often lead us *away* from home. That's what happened to my friend Susan.

Susan was single, successful in her career, and lonely. When she turned forty without any marriage prospects in sight, she consoled herself with a spending spree. She took a vacation every other month, purchased a fur, and even splurged on a Porsche. She had a great time, for a while. But soon enough, the car became a money pit, with the cost of maintenance straining her finances. Susan had hoped her purchases would help fill the void of loneliness. They didn't even come close. (We'll return to Susan's story in chapter 11.)

There's nothing wrong with nice cars and coats. But there's a lot that's wrong with looking to them to give our lives meaning and joy and with stretching our finances too far to buy them. That's what turns us into prodigals.

Unfortunately, many of us do what Susan did. We settle for temporary pleasures—*false desires*—masquerading as the sources of meaning, purpose, and joy. It's the primary reason so many people's financial lives are in such bad shape. Oh, they may look good on the outside, but debt, stress, and dissatisfaction often lurk just behind the façades of financial success and happiness.

Keeping Up Appearances

During my financial seminars, I always ask the participants to fill out anonymous surveys about their financial situation, and I'm always surprised by how many people say they are either "one paycheck from disaster" or "in crisis." It's usually at least one-quarter of the participants. Often, these are well-educated, well-dressed professionals—the picture of success. You'd think I'd be used to the disconnect between how people appear to be doing financially and how they're actually doing, but I'm not.

Our perceptions of people's financial condition are formed by what we see: the homes they live in, the cars they drive, the clothes they wear, and the happiness they seem to be enjoying. The reality includes things we don't usually see: how much debt they have, how much savings they don't have, how much stress they endure.

Think of the people you know. Aren't many of them living in nice homes, driving newer cars, wearing fashionable clothes, and looking happy? But what's the truth? Because we can't see beyond the surface and rarely talk with each other about money, we can't tell whether even our closest friends can actually *afford* their lifestyles. Nor do we know how much tension they live with behind closed doors.

The lifestyles of the people around us influence our own financial behaviors, and, unfortunately, perception usually wins out over reality. Our choices are shaped by how we *think* others are doing. We see our coworkers and neighbors enjoying new cars, nice clothes, and exciting vacations. Since we figure we're earning about what they're earning, we try to keep pace. Then we find ourselves perpetuating the illusion by presenting a certain public image—a financial front—with the car we drive, the home we live in, the clothes we wear, and even the happiness we convey.

The Pull of Our Profession

Sometimes our profession fosters overspending. This was true for a couple I met during a break in a seminar I was leading. Although drowning in debt, they were thinking about buying a new car and, apparently, hoping

I'd give them permission. The husband had become a real estate salesman, and they wondered how he could sell homes if he had to drive prospects around in anything less than a new luxury car. They were convinced his customers would expect him to drive such a car, so they saw no other option than to buy one, even if it meant going further into debt.

Sociologist Erving Goffman wrote about this tendency to accept the props that accompany certain social situations and professions. He observed, "When an actor takes on an established social role, usually he finds that a particular front has already been established for it."[5] The couple in my seminar believed that a nice car was a necessary prop if a person were to be successful as a real estate agent.

A lot of physicians believe something similar. One of the many surprising findings contained in *The Millionaire Next Door*, a research-based look at the financial habits of people with a net worth of $1 million or more, is that physicians tend to *under*-perform other high-income professionals in wealth accumulation. Part of this, authors Thomas Stanley and William Danko concluded, is beyond the doctors' control. Their extended schooling delays the start of their earning years. But some of it is well within their control. Many physicians put themselves in a precarious financial position early in their careers by purchasing big homes, expensive cars, and the best clothing—all out of a felt need to "play their parts" as doctors.[6] How could we possibly trust our tonsils to the care of someone who drives a five-year-old car and lives in a middle-class neighborhood? Never mind that most of us don't know what our doctors drive or where they live.

Of course, we don't need a prestigious profession or a high income to fall for the story that happiness is something we can buy.

The Pull of Our Culture

We are all subject to the influence of our culture, which tells us that joy is just one purchase away. For example, don't you often feel that you need something more in order to be happy? Perhaps you have your sights set on a new car. The one you purchased four years ago was great—for the first six months or so. It still runs just fine, but you're getting bored with it. You're thinking about trading up to a car with newer styling and more interesting features. You still owe a bit on your car, but the salesperson said you could roll that amount into a new loan, and if you opt for a longer payoff period, your payments wouldn't even be that much higher.

Many of us think like this. We want something, buy it, feel good about it for a while, start wanting a newer/better version, buy it, feel good about it for a while, start wanting a newer/better version, and on it goes. But, ultimately, it doesn't bring financial success or joy. In fact, frequent upgrading of our clothes, cars, and electronic gear often leaves us with low savings, heavy debt, and lingering dissatisfaction. It keeps us on the treadmill of wanting and buying and hoping the next purchase will bring us the happiness we long for.

Along with its overt message that spending leads to happiness, our culture sends us a subtle message that it is our *duty* to spend. The business pages of our newspapers describe upticks in household spending in positive terms—our economy is highly dependent upon such spending—and describe increases in savings in negative terms.

In fact, after the terrorist attacks of 9/11, our leaders told us that one of the best things we could do for our country was to go shopping. I remember reading a front-page story during a period of slow economic growth in which a top economist said that the thing that worried him the most was that people might start saving more. At first I thought I had misread his comment, so I read it again. Sure enough, he was concerned that people might start saving more of their money. From an economist's perspective, it makes sense. More savings equals less spending, and that's bad for our economy.

Of course, it is not our responsibility to prop up the economy. Nor do we need to allow our profession or marketing messages to dictate what we do with our dollars. We'll find greater financial success and satisfaction if we allow ourselves to be "pulled" down the path of our true desires.

The Pull of Our True Desires

Our world is filled with how-to advice doled out in easy-to-follow fashion: "Three simple steps to untold riches!" But this counsel too often sends us down a path that is neither productive nor satisfying. *In order to manage money successfully and joyfully, we must understand our true desires and make financial choices that are consistent with those longings.* It's the financial manifestation of what Parker Palmer calls living "divided no more"—deciding to "no longer act on the outside in a way that contradicts some truth about [ourselves] that [we] hold deeply on the inside."[7]

That was the decision an African-American seamstress from Montgomery, Alabama, made on a history-changing day in 1955 when she defied a racist city law requiring her to sit in the back of a city bus.

> Legend has it that . . . a graduate student came to Rosa Parks and asked, "Why did you sit down at the front of the bus that day?" Rosa Parks did not say that she sat down to launch a movement, because her motives were more elementary than that. She said, "I sat down because I was tired." But she did not mean that her feet were tired. She meant that her soul was tired, her heart was tired, her whole being was tired of playing by racist rules, of denying her soul's claim to selfhood."[8]

Many of us are tired as well. We're tired of playing by rules that leave us stuck in the unproductive and unfulfilling cycle of want, buy, and want some more. We're also tired of keeping up the appearance that all is well. It's taking too great a toll on our finances and our joy.

What all that means is that we've wandered from home, settled for too little. In order to find our way back, we need to understand how we got here in the first place.

WHAT TO REMEMBER

1. Within each of us are *true desires*—powerful, heartfelt longings for that which gives our lives meaning and joy.
2. When we're not clear about what really matters, we leave ourselves open to our culture's many suggestions as to what will make us happy. Our profession and especially our culture have a strong influence on us, often encouraging us to spend more than we should and buy things not consistent with what truly matters to us.
3. In order to manage money successfully and joyfully, we must understand our true desires and make financial choices that move us toward those longings.

WHAT TO DO

1. Make a list of some of your financial hopes, dreams, and goals. Use a piece of paper or the personal workbook (pages 22–24) to jot down some that most immediately come to mind. Think of some tangible goals (getting out of debt, saving for the down payment on a house) and also some emotional goals (feeling less stressed about money, more confident that you're on track toward the future you desire). You'll have a chance to refine your list in the chapters ahead.
2. List some of the "props" of your profession. Do your colleagues or others in your profession tend to drive certain vehicles, wear certain types or brands of clothing, or take certain types of vacations? Have you found yourself making similar choices? If so, how have the choices impacted your finances? Have they held you back from building savings or accomplishing other financial goals?
3. List some ways our culture—the culture at large (advertising, marketing) and also the culture that more closely surrounds you (your family, friends, coworkers, and neighbors)—has impacted

your financial choices. Write some of your thoughts on a piece of paper or in your workbook on page 25.

WHAT THE WORD SAYS

People look at the outside of a person, but the LORD looks at the heart. (1 Samuel 16:7, NCV)

Chapter 3

WHY WE'VE SETTLED FOR SO LITTLE

We accept the reality of the world with which we are presented.

— CHRISTOF, *THE TRUMAN SHOW*

What if this is as good as it gets?

— MELVIN UDALL, *AS GOOD AS IT GETS*

Why do we allow the misguided money-related messages of our culture to sway us so easily? Why do we find it difficult to avoid making financial choices that are not in our best interests? It's because something deep within us—*our financial identity*—enables those messages to connect with us. Each of us has a financial identity, a money-related worldview. Unfortunately, many of us have unintentionally settled for a financial identity that's inconsistent with who we were made to be. Even worse, most of us are unaware that we even have a financial identity, leaving it free to operate unchecked and unchallenged. But it's there, all right, and we ignore it at our peril, because our financial identity greatly influences our ability to achieve financial success and joy.

Survey Says . . .

To help you understand your financial identity, I'd like you to take a short quiz. As you read the following questions or statements, pay attention to the first answers that come to mind. Don't analyze them. Don't ask clarifying questions. Just go with your first thoughts. Here's the first question:

How much annual income does it take to raise a family today?

I know, I know. There are different-sized families and different costs of living in different parts of the country. As I said, don't overthink this. Just go with the first thought that comes to mind. How much annual income does it take to raise a family?

Now fill in the blank in the following statement:

A car should be replaced after it has _____ miles.

What do you think? How many miles?

To answer the final question, imagine that you've been called in to interview for your dream job. It's an incredible, once-in-a-lifetime opportunity. You look in your closet and realize you have nothing to wear. Not for this occasion. So now you're headed to your favorite clothing store to buy a new suit or outfit. Here's the question:

How much will you need to spend?

For guys, this question is usually straightforward. We just need a new suit—maybe a new shirt and tie as well. But for women, it can be more challenging. When I ask this in my seminars, at least one woman usually wants to know, "Does that include accessories?" Sure, throw in the accessories. What do you think? How much for a new suit or outfit?

What's the point of this quiz? To help you recognize that we all have money-related attitudes and assumptions. Problem is, we rarely articulate them. But they exist in all of us, living like the unquestioned truth, quietly guiding all manner of our financial decisions, big and small. Our attitudes, assumptions, beliefs, desires, and commitments about money-related issues collectively constitute our financial identity. Anyone who wants to manage money successfully and joyfully must answer this question: *Financially speaking, who am I?*

If we don't make a conscious choice about our financial identity, our culture will choose for us. And what identity do you think it will select?

I Spend, Therefore I Am

What label do marketers and government officials use to describe us? *Consumer*, right? It's a term we hear all the time: consumer sentiment, consumer confidence, consumer segments, consumer spending. We hear it so often you'll probably be surprised to learn its actual definition. To consume means to "spend wastefully," "use up," and "squander."[1] It comes from the Latin *consumere*, which means to "devour, waste, destroy."[2] Marketers would have us believe we are wasters and squanderers, people defined by our propensity to use stuff up. (Sounds a bit like the prodigal son, doesn't it?)

Even worse, the term *consumer* has come to mean those who look to the things they buy to shape their identity. At least that's how the chairman of one of the world's largest consumer products companies sees it:

> The brand defines the consumer. We are what we wear, what we eat, what we drive. Each of us . . . is a walking compendium of brands. The collection of brands we choose to assemble around us have become amongst the most direct expressions of our individuality — or more precisely, our deep psychological need to identify ourselves with others.[3]

I don't know about you, but I'd like to think my life is more than the sum total of what I wear, eat, and drive. However, when I read the research about our financial beliefs and behaviors, I see more than a few hints that we may have indeed settled for the identity of a *Consumer*, whether we meant to or not.

Many of us spend more than we make, living with low or no savings and high levels of debt; most of us *always* have something in mind that we look forward to buying;[4] almost half of us acknowledge thinking of our cars as a reflection of who we are;[5] and when asked about our biggest problem, our most frequent answer is "not having enough money."[6] Apparently, far from thinking of the love of money as "a root of all kinds of evil,"[7] most of us think the *lack* of money is the bigger problem.

The hopeful part of all this is that we were never meant to be *Consumers*. When God finished creating the heavens and the earth and everything in them, he didn't spend the sixth day making *Consumers* who would use up and waste all the stuff he created; he made human beings who were to work in his creation and care for it.[8] The *Consumer* is a cultural construct, an identity foisted on us a little over a hundred years ago. Here's a brief look at how the deal came down.

As the Culture Goes, So Go the People

The foundation of our consumer culture was established roughly between the 1880s and 1920s.[9] That's when many people moved from the country to the city and took up positions along assembly lines that mass-produced branded forms of everything from cars to clothing. Before then, people usually bought raw materials in bulk; there were no branded packages of ready-to-eat cereal and not much in the way of ready-to-wear clothing.[10]

The avalanche of products spilling off the assembly lines spawned department stores, which, in turn, spawned the increasingly sophisticated science of merchandising. Store managers learned to display items with an eye toward enticement.

The expansion of railway lines helped create national markets. The spread of telegraph and telephone lines helped create national advertising. With more goods to sell and more markets to reach, more aggressive promotional methods were needed. In 1916, a speaker told the Nashville Ad Club, "It is all very well to get the sales of things that people want to buy, but that is too small in volume. We must make people want many other things, in order to get the big increase in business."[11]

In the early years of the twentieth century, advertising moved beyond its heritage of matter-of-factly letting people know when and where products were available; it began encouraging people to *want* them. Historian Susan Strasser writes, "People who had never bought corn flakes were taught to need them; those formerly content to buy oats scooped from the grocer's bin were informed about why they should prefer Quaker Oats in a box."[12] Soon more sophisticated techniques for driving desire were developed: psychological techniques.

Historian William Leach notes, "By the 1910s American business was beginning to alter the meaning of goods through dramatic treatment, investing them with a significance that set them off and above other things . . . they attempted to give goods associative power," tying them to the notions of "glamour . . . luxury, escape, and adventure."[13] Boston College sociology professor Juliet Schor says the 1920s marked a turning point in the advertising industry:

> Of course, ads had been around for a long time. But something new was afoot, in terms of both scale and strategy. . . . Ads developed an association between the product and one's very identity. Eventually they came to promise everything and anything — from self-esteem, to status, friendship, and love.[14]

Any qualms people had about their ability to afford the items they now wanted were quickly allayed by the rapid rise of easy credit. Shoppers enjoyed the convenience of being able to charge their purchases, and merchants discovered that charge-account customers were both more impulsive in their spending and bigger spenders overall.[15]

The move from the country to the city marked far more than a change of address for people; it marked a change in their way of life and, soon enough, in their very identity. People went from farm work to factory work, from making things to buying things, and from self-sufficiency to income dependency. Susan Strasser writes, "Formerly *customers*, purchasing the objects of daily life from familiar craftspeople and storekeepers,

Americans became *consumers*."[16]

Businesses needed their customers to begin seeing themselves as consumers. Advertising historian Roland Marchand observed that success in business began to depend on "the nurture of qualities like wastefulness, self-indulgence, and artificial obsolescence."[17] According to William Leach, marketers began positioning the activities of consumption as being in the best interests of those doing the consuming: "The cardinal features of this culture were acquisition and consumption as the means of achieving happiness."[18] The high-consumption culture born during this era promoted what religion historian Joseph Haroutunian calls "'being' through 'having.'"[19]

Over the years, marketing has only gotten more prevalent and sophisticated. Advertising messages now blanket virtually every public space and are embedded in television shows, movies, video games, Broadway plays, novels, comic books, and more (there has even been talk of putting giant ads in outer space).[20] Today, when our friends recommend a product, we have to wonder if they're being paid for their point of view by one of the many buzz-marketing firms that have thousands of people chatting up products to their family, friends, and coworkers. Of course, this huge marketing system tends to be short on such messages as "Be sure to save for your retirement" and "Don't take out too large a mortgage." Instead, they tell us that the product being pitched will give us what we desire: a mate if we drive the right car, the skills of the latest basketball superstar if we buy the shoes he endorses, and on it goes. The marketers promise lasting happiness but, at best, deliver only temporary pleasure.

This is not to say we are defenseless against the powers of our consumer culture. We still have the power to choose. But it's easier to choose well when we see that what's behind the curtain of our consumer culture is a sophisticated system designed to foster financial beliefs and behaviors that may not be in our best interests.

A Consumer's Guiding Beliefs

The *Consumer* identity has two primary manifestations: the *Shopper* and the *Stockpiler*. The *Shopper*, by far the more common of the two, believes,

"A little more money will solve my problems" and "My value and happiness depend on what I own." The *Stockpiler* believes, "More money in savings or investments will bring more security."

Fear motivates both types. *Shoppers* fear not *being* enough without the next purchase; *Stockpilers* fear not *having* enough without the next deposit. *Shoppers* believe they need to *buy* more in order to be worthy; *Stockpilers* believe they need to *save or invest* more in order to be wealthy.

I was a classic *Shopper*. When I was getting myself into debt I was single, and it's embarrassing to think back on the ways I tried to impress dates by taking them to restaurants I could not afford. I also developed a prideful attitude, as if I had earned the money I received from my uncle. I lived in a high-rise in Chicago with a bus stop right outside the building's front door, but I never took the bus. If I had to go somewhere that didn't involve driving my car, I'd opt for a cab. I wasted a lot of money trying to live up to the image of the person I wanted to be, fearing that without the lavish lifestyle, I wouldn't be worthy of anyone's affection or esteem.

In contrast, Maria is a classic *Stockpiler*. Just thirty years old, she has already amassed a net worth of more than $250,000—on a salary of $45,000. To build wealth she often accepts overtime assignments that stretch her workweek to sixty-five hours, and she's rigorous about minimizing her spending. Although her net worth puts her in the top 5 percent of people in her age group, she does not feel secure. In fact, even though she is single, she worries about paying for college for the children she hopes to have one day.

For *Shoppers* and *Stockpilers*, the word of choice is *more*. Both are in a race in which the finish line keeps getting pushed back. *Shoppers* never have enough stuff; happiness always requires one more purchase. Their overspending results in a lack of savings and a heavy debt load. One missed paycheck or unexpected car repair can spell disaster. *Stockpilers*, on the other hand, never have enough savings; security always requires more in the bank. *Stockpilers* may be financially successful, but they have little freedom to enjoy their money because of their insatiable need for more; the fear of a market downturn leaves them anxious.

Psychologists have studied our quest for more—more than we have now and more than others have—and they've concluded that even when we get "more," it usually delivers far *less* happiness than we had hoped for. The problem with wanting more than we have now is that as we acquire more, we quickly get used to it and find ourselves wanting still more. Psychologists call this *adaptation*; economists call it *declining marginal utility* and the *hedonic treadmill*. As researcher Ronald Inglehart puts it, "In the long run, neither an ice cream cone nor a new car nor becoming rich and famous produces the same feelings of delight that it initially did. . . . Happiness is not the result of being rich, but a temporary consequence of having recently become richer."[21]

Think of your household electronics. Maybe you can remember the thrill of owning your first television, even though it had only a thirteen-inch screen. But that soon became ordinary, so you replaced it with a larger-screen television. That seemed like a big upgrade, and it provided much enjoyment—that is, until flat-screen televisions came on the market. Yours has been working out nicely, but the latest televisions are equipped with . . . And on it goes.

Basing our happiness on the other type of "more"—having more than other people have—is also a zero-sum game. Researchers call this *social comparison*. You and I know it as *keeping up with the Joneses*. Today we may be satisfied with our five-year-old Toyota Camry. But tomorrow when our neighbors show up in their new Avalon, with its leather seats and concert-quality stereo system, the old Camry just doesn't cut it anymore.

Juliet Schor points out that we may not be aware of the comparisons we make to other people. "It may be as simple as the fact that exposure to their latest 'lifestyle upgrade' plants the seed in our own mind that we must have it, too—whether it be a European vacation, this year's fashion statement, or piano lessons for the children."[22]

An Old Game

Our tendency to compare what we have with what others have is far from new. It's been a problem for so long that coveting is even one of the sins

God singles out in the Ten Commandments.[23] Yet we continue to play the comparison game, and we continue to lose, for someone else always has more. This goes a long way toward explaining why the number of people feeling "very happy" hasn't grown.

That's not to say there's no connection between money and happiness. Research proves that for those who move from poverty to the middle class, happiness increases a lot. However, beyond that, the happiness meter barely moves at all. According to Harvard psychology professor Daniel Gilbert, "Americans who earn $50,000 per year are much happier than those who earn $10,000 per year, but Americans who earn $5 million per year are not much happier than those who earn $100,000 per year."[24]

Is it possible to break this cycle of looking for happiness in all the wrong places? Is there any way to get off the *more* treadmill? Absolutely. We can do so by brushing up on our self-knowledge and familiarizing ourselves with what truly matters. Those insights will point the way home. The next two chapters are devoted to doing just that.

WHAT TO REMEMBER

1. Our culture would have us believe we are *Consumers*. By definition, to be a *Consumer* is to "spend wastefully," "use up," and "squander."

2. The *Consumer* identity has two manifestations: *Shoppers*, who look to what they buy for happiness, and *Stockpilers*, who look to the size of their savings or investment accounts for security.

3. *Consumers* want *more*—either more than they have now or more than others have. But the quest for more than we have now, whether things or savings, is futile because we quickly adapt to what we have and just as quickly find ourselves wanting more. The quest for more than others have fails as well because someone else always has more.

WHAT TO DO

1. Begin to notice the use of the term *Consumer*. Where do you see or hear it? How is it used?
2. Which manifestation of the *Consumer* identity do you relate to more — the *Shopper* or the *Stockpiler*? Write down some ways you see that manifestation impacting your use of money.
3. Consider the ways in which you have felt the need for more. Do you get bored with what you have? Or do you feel as though you don't have nice enough versions of what you own? With what types of things do you feel this the most? Your car? Your furniture? Your clothing? Do you really *need* more?

WHAT THE WORD SAYS

Don't copy the behavior and customs of this world, but let God transform you into a new person by changing the way you think. (Romans 12:2, NLT)

Part Two

Where We Belong

Listen to me, my children! Be wise and have enough sense to follow the right path.

— PROVERBS 23:19 (CEV)

He came to his senses.

— LUKE 15:17

Chapter 4

What Truly Matters

Love one another.

— JOHN 13:34

*Joy can be real only if people look upon their life as a
service, and have a definite object in life outside themselves
and their personal happiness.*

— LEO TOLSTOY

M ore than one hundred years ago, sociologist Georg Simmel observed people's use of money and concluded that, in many cases, it was leading them away from the sense of meaning and purpose they so desperately wanted. The reason, he felt, is that they simply didn't know what made for a meaningful, purposeful life: "The lack of something definite at the centre of the soul impels us to search for momentary satisfaction in ever-new stimulations, sensations and external activities."[1]

The path toward home will come into view only when we become clear about what truly matters—what really gives our lives meaning, purpose, and joy. As we saw in the last chapter, our culture has strong opinions about this. Researchers in the emerging field of positive psychology have had a lot to say on this topic as well, but their conclusions are quite different from those of our culture. And, as we'll see, the findings from psychology simply echo what the Bible has been teaching for thousands of years, beginning with our desire for meaningful relationships.

Relationships Matter

My parents passed away within twelve months of each other. The last year of my mother's life and the year that followed, which led to my father's death, was a time of much stress and sorrow. It was agonizing to see the pain that cancer inflicted on my mother and the debilitating effects of heart disease on my father. Making matters worse for my dad was the deep grief and loneliness he felt following the loss of my mother. They were married for nearly forty-seven years.

But that period was also a time of rich moments spent in simple conversation. I will always remember my father telling me in the quiet of a hospital room late one evening how grateful he was that my mom "took a chance" on him and that being married to her was his greatest joy. Living a little over an hour away from their house, I was able to spend a lot of time with them as their health declined, and it was one of my greatest honors to be at their side when they each drew their final breath. Throughout their illnesses, I saw firsthand what I think we all know to be true: When our time here draws to a close, our hearts will not be filled with longings to redecorate the living room or take one more trip to Europe; we'll simply want to be with the people we love. There's something about knowing that our time is short that helps us clarify what really matters.

Our culture encourages us to love money and what it can buy. Psychologists say if it's a life of meaning, purpose, and joy we're after, we'd be better off loving people. Social psychologist David Myers has reviewed hundreds of studies about happiness and concludes that "social support—feeling liked, affirmed, and encouraged by intimate friends and family—promotes both health and happiness." He cites numerous studies showing that people in close relationships cope better with various stresses, including bereavement, job loss, and illness. In one study of eight hundred college graduates, those who preferred a high income, occupational success, and prestige to having close friends and a close marriage were twice as likely to describe themselves as "fairly" or "very" unhappy.[2]

Of course, the research from psychology only affirms what the Bible teaches. Jesus taught that loving others is second only to loving God in importance.[3] And the apostle Paul said, "No matter what I say, what I believe, and what I do, I'm bankrupt without love."[4] We were made for relationships. It's written throughout the pages of Scripture.

The Money/Relationships Connection

What does our true desire for meaningful relationships have to do with money? Quite a bit, for the way we use money can either enhance our relationships or detract from them.

My friend Tom provides a good example of how our use of money can build our relationships. He and his wife, Rachel, committed early in their marriage to live free of debt. Not just credit card debt, but automobile and even mortgage debt as well. They figured the freer they were from debt, the freer they would be to spend time with the children they hoped to have. When Tom and Rachel decided to buy a home, they looked for one that was large enough for the family they desired and affordable enough to pay off in a short amount of time. They found just the home in a western suburb of Chicago. It had plenty of space and was located near a riverside trail, which appealed to their love of running and biking. It was also reasonably priced, partly because it had no garage. They were willing to make the trade-off: no garage in exchange for a house that, before long, would require no mortgage payments.

Rather than relying on the advice of real estate agents or mortgage brokers, who would have told them that they could afford a much more expensive home, Tom and Rachel made their decision based on what truly matters: their commitment to family relationships. By living well beneath their means, they paid off their house in just five years. That enabled Tom to reduce his hours at work and be content with the lower pay that came with the deal so he could spend more time at home, which is especially important now that they have five children.

Unfortunately, not every couple is so naturally in sync when it comes to finances, and this can put stress on the marriage relationship. A former coworker once confided that he and his wife were having frequent arguments about money. They were "not on the same page" financially, he explained. She wanted to do some significant landscaping in their yard and pay for it by taking out extra money when they refinance their home. He wasn't as comfortable taking on more debt.

As we talked more about it over lunch, it became clear that this couple did not see money management as a partnership. Although they had a budget, he kept the books, while she wondered why there wasn't enough for the things she'd like.

I suggested that they begin holding monthly "board of directors" meetings. The purpose for the first couple of meetings would be to pray about, discuss, and develop a financial vision for their family. (What is God calling them to do with the resources he has blessed them with? Do they have enough in an emergency fund? Should they plan to help their children pay for college? What do they see themselves doing in their later years?) From that vision, they could set specific goals, and those goals would make daily financial choices much clearer.

It may be that the decision to invest in making their backyard more inviting fits perfectly with a shared vision to spend more quality family time at home. And maybe they could move toward each other—agreeing to invest in the landscaping, but waiting until they have enough in savings to pay for it without going into debt. Or they may find that the landscaping project would prevent them from accomplishing a more important goal. If that's the case, saying no to the landscaping project is likely to become easier since they both agree that the other goal is a higher priority.

Letting Relationships Lead

Who are some of the most important people in your life? If you are single, it might be your parents, siblings, and closest friends. If you're married, your spouse is probably at the top of the list. If you have children, I'm sure they're on the list as well. Who else? Get a clear picture in your mind of at least five people who are really important to you. Now ask yourself whether your use of money is strengthening these relationships or hindering them in some way.

It's all too easy to buy the house we want, even though it requires such a long commute that we have little time to spend with family or friends. It's just as easy to spend so much on clothing or vacations that we go into debt or try to get by without savings, even if doing so adds stress to our relationships.

That's why, whether single or married, it's important to ask how your financial decisions are likely to impact your most significant relationships. For example:

- Would that cross-country move that comes with a $10,000 raise be in your best interest, or would saying good-bye to your friends be too much to exchange for the higher pay?
- Would a house with more space best serve your family, or would living with more financial margin be a better choice?
- Do you really need to be able to tap the Internet, watch television, and check e-mail with your cell phone, or would the financial breathing space of a less-expensive calling plan help you save for vacations with family or friends?

It's not inherently wrong to relocate with your company, buy a bigger house, or opt for the latest cell phone services. But it's important to ask and wrestle with such questions because relationships matter more than we sometimes realize.

So does contribution.

Contribution Matters

In the opening scene of *About Schmidt*, Warren Schmidt, played by Jack Nicholson, is staring at a clock on the wall of his office, counting down the minutes before his final day at work will be over and his retirement will begin. He has spent his career working as an actuary for an insurance company, where he rose to the position of assistant vice president. At the end of his last day, Schmidt sits in the midst of his boxed belongings, watching the clock, waiting until 5:00 p.m., when the workday and his career will be over.

At a retirement dinner that evening, a longtime colleague toasts him, telling Schmidt he should feel "rich" to have devoted his life to something so meaningful. The look on Schmidt's face says he's not so sure. He once dreamed of having his own business but instead chose the security of a steady paycheck.

Shortly after Schmidt's retirement, his wife dies. The sudden changes — retirement, the loss of his wife of more than forty years — leave Schmidt wondering even more about the meaning of his life. "I know we're all pretty small in the big scheme of things," he writes to Ndugu, a six-year-old Tanzanian orphan he sponsors in response to a television advertisement. "And I suppose the most you can hope for is to make some kind of difference, but what kind of difference have I made? What in the world is better because of me?"

Our culture would have us believe that life is about *competition*. It tells us that happiness is found in having more than we have now and more than others have. But as Nicholson's character expresses so well, it's *contribution* that we long for, a sense that we are making a difference with our lives. David Myers says that when our work adds purpose to our lives, when we view it as a calling, it adds mightily to the quality of our lives: "Happiness is loving what you do, and knowing it matters."[5] Here again, psychology affirms the biblical teaching that we were designed to make a difference — that God "created us for a life of good deeds."[6]

The Money/Contribution Connection

We can experience a sense of calling in our paid work, our volunteer work, the work of parenting, and more. Martin Seligman, a psychology professor at the University of Pennsylvania, says that for some people, meaning is found simply in how they view their work. He tells of a hospital orderly who meticulously selected pictures for the walls of a room where a close friend of Seligman's lay unconscious. The orderly explained, "I'm responsible for the health of all these patients. Take Mr. Miller here. He hasn't woken up since they brought him in, but when he does, I want to make sure he sees beautiful things right away."[7]

This orderly viewed his work as integral to the healing of patients. Another orderly might think of his work as menial and meaningless. The first orderly sees his job as a calling; the second sees it as a source of income. The tasks are the same; only the perspective is different.

Other people find meaning in how they use the fruits of their labors. For as long as Michelle can remember, she has cared about the poor. When she was young, she considered a career in social work, but her father talked her into studying business, and she became a certified public accountant. Then her brother persuaded her to go to law school, and she became a corporate attorney. It's never been her dream job, but she excels at it and earns a good living. She has thought about leaving the corporate world to work in the nonprofit sector, but she candidly acknowledges feeling afraid of leaving something she knows how to do so well. So Michelle has found a way to make a meaningful contribution without leaving her day job.

For several years, she has invested her skills and money in an organization that serves homeless people in Chicago. Michelle chooses to live a far-less-expensive lifestyle than many of her colleagues in order to give away a remarkable 35 percent of her income—some of it to her church, much of it to the homeless ministry. Soon the ministry will open a new youth and family center where neighborhood kids will receive after-school tutoring and take part in sports leagues and other programs designed to help them stay out of gangs and finish school. Michelle used her legal skills to help the organization complete a deal with the city of Chicago to purchase land for the center, and her donations helped fund it.

Michelle says that investing her money, time, and talents in the homeless ministry is one of the most rewarding parts of her life. "I know that this ministry is changing people's lives. People are getting off drugs, getting back on their feet. Volunteers are mentoring kids who've never had positive role models in their lives. Being part of this helps me see a greater purpose for my career path."

While Michelle's use of her money and talents enables her to make a meaningful contribution, other people's use of money prevents them from doing so. For example, a heavy debt load keeps some folks from pursuing the vocation best suited to their gifts and passions because the work doesn't pay enough to cover the bills they've incurred. Others have become so acclimated to their lifestyle that it seems unrealistic to go from full-time work to part-time work in order to pursue their true calling, which could be spending more time with their children.

As Po Bronson points out, "Failure's hard, but success is far more dangerous. If you're successful at the wrong thing, the mix of praise and money and opportunity can lock you in forever."[8] It's not easy to make a change, particularly when things are going well—you keep getting promoted, the money is plentiful, the slaps on the back frequent. In many ways, that was my story.

I was working a corporate job with a good salary and plenty of perks. The position enabled me to provide a comfortable life for my family. But I felt a growing sense of unease, a mounting conviction that there was something else I was meant to do. It wasn't easy to push back from the corporate table, where the food was plentiful. And I took some flak from well-meaning people who questioned the timing of my decision to step down. They wondered whether it would be more responsible to wait until our kids were grown before following my dream to write and teach full-time. But I couldn't ignore the disconnect between my career and my heart. I felt like I was "living divided," and I just couldn't do it anymore.

I'm blessed that from the earliest days of our marriage, my wife shared my dream of my being able to do this work full-time someday. Together, we made decisions designed to help us save enough money for me to be able to walk away from my corporate job. We both worked at the start of our marriage, but we committed to living on one income so that we could give to causes we believed in, save aggressively, and be prepared to have Jude stay home with the children we hoped to have. When we bought our first home, a condo, it was in what Realtors optimistically termed an "up-and-coming" Chicago neighborhood. Basically, that meant three things: There was no Starbucks down the block, the symbols that would often appear overnight on the corner mailbox were not meant to beautify the neighborhood, and we were able to live with plenty of margin. I drove the car I brought into our marriage until it had nearly 200,000 miles on it. Now I drive the car Jude brought into the marriage, and it has 160,000 miles. During my corporate career, we could have easily bought a nice luxury car for cash, but the freedom to pursue this work mattered more, so we focused on building savings.

It's all too easy to lose touch with our longing to make a meaningful contribution. Before you know it, the house payment, the car payment, and the hours you work to pay for it all can make any thought of pursuing more meaningful work seem unrealistic. Or it's easy to succumb to fear. You think, *How will I make it work if I choose a line of work that pays less?* Even worse, *What if I fail?* But consider this: What if you never try? Wouldn't that be the greater failure? If there's an ache in your heart to do something else, pay attention to that ache; it'll motivate you to do what it takes to pursue the work you were meant to do. And that will help you recapture some of the passion you once had.

Don't Be a Bystander in the Passion Game

Some people cry while watching love stories. I cried while watching *Walk the Line*, the story of Johnny Cash. A number of scenes stirred my heart, but especially the concert Cash performed at Folsom Prison toward the end of the movie. Just before going on stage, he saw something that reminded him of his brother, who died in an accident when he was very young. That memory kindled something in Cash—perhaps a mix of grief, anger, and maybe even a haunting question about whether he could have done something to prevent his brother's death. It all poured out on stage. His performance was that of a man living life to the full, unable to hold anything back. The energy he brought to that performance overwhelmed me. As the credits rolled and the lights came up, I felt embarrassed that my eyes were glistening with tears. But mostly, I was glad to be that moved. Something in me longed to live with the passion I saw before me.

A few weeks later, I read this comment about Johnny Cash from the musician Don McLean: "One of the things I loved about him was he was a little frightening when you first heard him."[9] Isn't that great? Isn't that exactly what it's like when we see someone bringing all he has to whatever he's doing?

Performers don't have the exclusive rights to passion. If you work at something you believe in, something that makes a difference in the world, something that's an expression of who you are and what you were put here to do, won't you do it with passion? Isn't life far too short to settle for anything less?

Letting Contribution Lead

What contribution do you long to make with your life? When it's all said and done, what difference will you want to have made? Maybe the off-road adventure you long to pursue is that vocational dream that comes to mind every time life gets quiet enough for you to notice — the one you keep trying to hush because of your financial obligations. What if you began using your money in a way that could make your dream job come true? What if you had enough savings to quit your current job or reduce your hours or go back to school in order to pursue the work you really want to do? Your employer might even pay for your schooling. The vast majority of large employers offers some type of educational assistance, yet fewer than 10 percent of eligible employees take advantage of such programs.[10] Does your employer offer tuition reimbursement? If so, why aren't you taking advantage of it?

So what if saving money to pursue the work you were meant to do means vacationing a bit closer to home or wearing last year's clothes another year? If those sacrifices enabled you to pursue more meaningful work, wouldn't they be worth it? The ads promise that the seaside resort and this year's fashions will make your life so much more exciting, but the truth is, doing what it takes to pursue more meaningful work will be the route to a far more satisfying adventure.

It's all too easy to use money in a way that moves you further away from your longing to make a difference — further and further away from home. It's all too easy to take on financial obligations that rob you of the flexibility to accept a job for less pay, even if it's the one that resonates with your heart. So as you contemplate each of your many financial choices, ask yourself how your choices are likely to impact your ability to pursue the work you were meant to do. (If you are married, be sure to do this in partnership with your spouse.)

For example:

- How would remodeling the kitchen — along with the monthly payments on the home equity loan you plan to use to pay for it — impact your ability to pursue the work you long to do? Might it just chain you to your cubicle for the next five years?
- Would taking a promotion that's been offered to you be the wisest choice, or could the extra hours required by the job kill any chance of going back to school or doing the volunteer work you want to do?
- Do you really need two cars, or would the ability to build a sabbatical fund make the inconveniences of living with just one worth the effort?

To be sure, these are not easy choices. It is not inherently wrong to opt for the new kitchen, the promotion, or the dual-car household. But if the choices diminish your ability to live a life of meaning and joy, are they really worth it? It's important to at least consider such questions.

Our Greatest True Desire

As we have seen, two elements of what truly matters in life are having meaningful relationships and making a meaningful contribution. Both are part of our design; they're part of who we are. When we make financial choices that strengthen our relationships and help us make a difference with our lives, we're on the path toward home.

But within each of us is a third longing. In fact, it is the most important one, for when we understand this true desire, we see once and for all that we were never meant to settle for life as *Consumers*; we were meant to be so much more.

WHAT TO REMEMBER

1. Two of our most important true desires are the desire for meaningful relationships and the desire to make a meaningful contribution with our lives.
2. Successful, joyful money management involves making financial choices that support these desires.
3. Such choices look different for different people, but we can stay on track by asking ourselves such questions as: Will buying a home with more space enhance our family relationships, or could it hurt them if we stretch our finances too far in buying the home?

WHAT TO DO

1. Who are the most important people in your life? Take the time right now to write them down on a piece of paper or in your workbook, but try to include no more than five. To make it easier, group some together. For example, if you have kids, don't list each one separately; just write down "my children." Do the same with your parents and other important groups of people in your life.
2. What contributions do you long to make with your life? Are there causes you'd like to support with either your volunteer time or your money? What did you once long to do that you have given up on because there are bills to pay? Would you like to switch from full-time work to part-time work so you can spend more time with your children? Capture some of your thoughts on paper. Don't worry about "how" just yet. We'll get to that later. For now, just focus on "what."
3. Now take a look at the list of financial goals you wrote down at the end of chapter 2. How might the pursuit and accomplishment of each goal impact your most valued relationships and your ability to make the difference with your life that you want to make? See if you can identify at least one way that the pursuit

and accomplishment of each goal could be helpful and at least one way that it might be a hindrance. Write your answers on a piece of paper or in the workbook. Are there any changes you'd like to make to your goals list?

WHAT THE WORD SAYS

Love others as much as you love yourself. (Matthew 22:39, CEV)

We are God's workmanship, created in Christ Jesus to do good works, which God prepared in advance for us to do. (Ephesians 2:10)

Chapter 5

WHAT MATTERS MOST

*The Quaker teacher Douglas Steere was fond of saying the
ancient human question "Who am I?" leads inevitably to
the equally important question "Whose am I?" — for there
is no self outside of relationship.*

— PARKER PALMER

*Anyone who belongs to Christ has become a new person.
The old life is gone; a new life has begun!*

— 2 Corinthians 5:17 (NLT)

I used to play golf fairly frequently — at least once a week, sometimes
more. I kept up on the latest equipment and often spent my lunch hour
hitting balls on a driving range. These days I hardly play at all. I'm in a
season of life, with young children and a new career, that doesn't leave me
with the wide swaths of free time required for a round of golf.

For a while, the less I played, the less I seemed to miss it. But then
I took my friend Tom up on his offer to join him for a round of golf on
his birthday, and all that I love about the game came flooding back. Just
putting my clubs in the trunk of my car filled me with an excitement I
hadn't felt in some time. When I got to the course, smelling the freshly
cut grass and hearing the sound of golf balls being struck on the practice
range sent an indescribable happiness coursing through my veins.

What gives you great joy? Maybe you love to garden. You subscribe
to magazines about gardening, and you've invested considerable time and

money in a backyard oasis that soothes your soul. Maybe you get great enjoyment from your vocation. It makes a difference in the world and is deeply satisfying. Or maybe there's a special place where you vacation each year. The beauty of the place and the memories you've built there fill you with a rich sense of joy.

We all long to spend more time doing the things that give us the greatest happiness. Each is a gift to be cherished. But C. S. Lewis gently encourages us to open our eyes a bit wider and see that our healthy desires for such things are but expressions of an even greater desire.

> It (is) not *in* them, it only comes through them and what (comes) through them (is) longing. . . . For they are not the thing itself; they are only the scent of a flower we have not found, the echo of a tune we have not heard, news from a country we have never visited.[1]

In other words, each of our greatest longings is really a longing for God.[2] This doesn't mean we should try to dampen our desire for what gives us great joy, were that even possible. Gerald May makes a critical distinction when he differentiates between "freedom *from* desire" and "freedom *of* desire."[3] Freedom *from* desire involves pretending that our hearts don't exist. Freedom *of* desire is yearning to do the things we most love to do, all the while knowing that the *deepest* desire of our hearts is the desire for God.

Within this realization lies the opportunity to completely alter our relationship with money. When we know that even our best experiences with the things of this world will not—indeed, cannot—fulfill our deepest longings, we gain a new freedom to enjoy them for what they are: good gifts from God, but not the basis of our identity, value, security, or ultimate happiness. As John Eldredge puts it, we express our longing for God best when we "enjoy what there is now to enjoy, while waiting with eager anticipation for the feast to come."[4]

Faith Matters

Our consumer culture would have us believe that life is all about us — our comfort, our pleasure. It says the path toward happiness is marked "more": more money, more stuff, more wanting and buying and wanting again. But psychologists beg to differ. They say the me-first philosophy is not the path to a satisfying life. University of Pennsylvania psychologist Martin Seligman, author of *Authentic Happiness*, writes, "A meaningful life is one that joins with something larger than we are,"[5] and, "The larger the entity to which you can attach yourself, the more meaning in your life."[6] Of course, there is no "entity" larger than God.

In the previous chapter, we discussed two of our true desires: our desire for meaningful relationships and our desire to make a meaningful contribution with our lives. Our third true desire — in fact, our greatest longing — is our desire for relationship with God. Blaise Pascal wrote, "In a soul that will live forever, there is an infinite void that nothing can fill, but an infinite unchangeable being."[7]

In the midst of our noisy consumer culture, the God of the universe invites us into a relationship with him: "Come to me, all you who are weary and burdened, and I will give you rest."[8] The Bible says that when we accept that invitation, we gain a new identity. We become "a new creation; the old has gone, the new has come!"[9] When we enter into a relationship with Christ, we become "children of God."[10] The implications are far-reaching. Even if we focus on only the financial implications, they are profound, for they hold the key to freeing us from the lie that our value and security are based on money and what it can buy.

Consumers with a *Shopper* perspective believe they need to constantly earn their value through the products and brands they buy. But the Bible says, "Life is not measured by how much one owns."[11] As children of God, we are fully loved just as we are. We don't need to drive the right car or wear the right clothes. It's okay if we *do* drive the right car or wear the right clothes. We have the freedom to choose them. In fact, the Bible says that God gives us things, in part, for our enjoyment.[12] But here's the critical difference: As fully loved sons and daughters of God, we no longer *need* such things. Our identity, value, and happiness no longer depend on them.

Consumers with a *Stockpiler* perspective believe they need to constantly increase their security through the money they put in savings and investments. But the Bible says that it's foolish to look to our wealth for security.[13] It also tells us that God knows our needs and has promised to provide for us.[14] That doesn't mean we aren't to save. In fact, the Bible clearly teaches us to save[15] (a topic we'll cover in chapter 7). But here's the critical difference: As fully loved sons and daughters of God, we no longer need to obsess over how much we have in savings. Our security is not based on how much we have in the bank.

The Money/Faith Connection

So how do we manage our relationships with God and money? While Jesus said that we cannot serve both,[16] the Bible does not say that money is evil. In fact, I believe 1 Timothy 6:10 is one of the most misquoted verses in the entire Bible. Many people think it says that money is the root of all evil. It doesn't. It warns against "the *love of* money" (emphasis added). It isn't money that's the problem; it's our heart attitude about money; it's allowing money to take precedence over God.

In the parable of the talents, Jesus depicts the ideal way to relate to God and money. In the story, God is a wealthy landowner who goes on a journey and temporarily entrusts his property to his servants. Eventually, he returns and checks to see what they have done with all he has entrusted to them.

This parable establishes some key insights that can help us use money in a God-honoring manner. First, God owns everything.[17] We may have the title for our house or car, but everything in our possession simply has been temporarily entrusted to us. Second, God cares about what we do with what he gives us, and he expects us to do something productive with it. When the master returned, he had strong words of affirmation for the two servants who had successfully invested his money.

Clearly, God does not want us to waste or squander what he entrusts to us. That means there is no such thing as a *Christian Consumer*; it's an oxymoron. What, then, *is* our financial identity? Most biblical money management teachers use the term *steward*, which, by definition, means someone who manages property belonging to someone else. We hear that word a lot in church circles, so much so that it may be misunderstood. We might think of it in terms of us loaning our home to some friends while we're on vacation. We would expect our friends to be good stewards—to leave it in the same condition as when we loaned it to them; we certainly wouldn't expect them to build an addition while we're gone.

But according to the parable of the talents, we are to do more than just "take care" of what God has given us. Look at what happened to the third servant. He didn't squander what had been entrusted to him on wild living. He simply returned it in the exact condition it was given to him. And for that he was harshly rebuked.[18] It seems that we are to take all that has been entrusted to us—money, time, skills, passions—and put it to productive, God-glorifying use.

Perhaps a more helpful way of viewing our financial identity is to see ourselves as *Builders*. Jesus used the builder metaphor when he said,

> Everyone who hears these words of mine and puts them into practice is like a wise man who built his house on the rock. The rain came down, the streams rose, and the winds blew and beat against that house; yet it did not fall, because it had its foundation on the rock.[19]

The apostle Paul used the builder metaphor as well when he said, "Each one should be careful how he builds. For no one can lay any foundation other than the one already laid, which is Jesus Christ."[20]

When we place our faith in Christ, our relationship with him becomes the foundation of our lives and therefore the foundation of our financial lives. Our old *Consumer* identity has gone; our new *Builder* identity has come. The *Consumer* identity is destructive; it's about wasting, squandering, and using up. The *Builder* identity is constructive; it's about building into our relationships, creating lives of meaningful contribution, and honoring God in all that we do.

Consumers believe life is all about them; *Builders* know that life is all about God. *Consumers* believe money and things matter; *Builders* know that people matter. *Consumers* are all about competition; *Builders* are all about contribution. *Consumers* seek happiness but find only short-term pleasures; *Builders* seek to glorify God, finding lasting joy.

Builders understand that this life is not all there is. It's the polar opposite of the perspective promoted in our consumer culture, which says this life *is* all there is and offers our only hope for happiness. The apostle Paul mocked the consumerist live-for-today philosophy when he said, "Let us eat and drink, for tomorrow we die."[21] The belief that this life is all there is—in essence, this is as good as it gets—is what prompts some people to take on too much debt as they impatiently grab for all that they can now. It's why so many people settle for the lies that they are *Consumers* and that what they buy will give their lives meaning, purpose, and joy. It's what leaves them working for that which does not satisfy.[22]

It's hard to see this as we walk through stores with signs screaming "Buy Now" and "Instant Financing Available," but we were made to live with more patience, with hope that is set further into the future. The Bible says that God has "set eternity in the human heart."[23] We were made to hold the things of this world with open hands of gratitude, knowing that all we have has been temporarily entrusted to us by our loving God, not with the clenched fists of entitlement. Such patience comes from an identity and financial worldview built on a foundation of faith.

Not Just About Successful Money Management

Looking to money and what it can buy for our identity, value, and security isn't just a bad idea—it doesn't just hinder our quest for financial success and happiness. It is what the Bible calls sin. When Jesus was asked which commandment is the most important, he answered, "Love the Lord your God with all your heart and with all your soul and with all your mind."[24] Don't you love the bottom-line nature of his answer? Poets and philosophers have pondered the purpose of our lives throughout the ages, and here's the answer in a simple sentence: Love God. It's the manifestation of God's Old Testament commandment to "have no other gods before me."[25] Anytime we put money, material things, or anything else before our relationship with God, we sin.

Rembrandt painted a powerful depiction of the return of the prodigal son, showing him kneeling before his father. The son's shoes are worn to the point of falling off, his clothes dirty rags, his sorrow overwhelming. He knows that his actions have been more than merely misguided: "Father, I have *sinned* against heaven and against you. I am no longer worthy to be called your son."[26]

In Henri Nouwen's insightful meditation on that painting and the biblical story on which it is based, he wrote, "At issue here is the question: 'To whom do I belong? To God or to the world? . . . I am the prodigal son every time I search for unconditional love where it cannot be found.'"[27] Indeed, anytime we search for our value or security in money and what it can buy, we wander from home as prodigal sons and daughters.

But here's the good news. Just as the father in the parable of the prodigal son waited patiently to welcome and embrace his son when he finally did come home, God is waiting patiently for all who are apart from him, eager to welcome them home.[28]

Where are you on your spiritual journey? Maybe you're at the beginning, wondering if there is a God and, if there is, what changes may come if you place your faith in him. You're standing on the edge of commitment, but fear or uncertainty is holding you back. Or maybe you *believe* in God, but it's head knowledge; you have not fully turned your life over to him.

When I was first exploring matters of faith, I learned there's a distinction between *believing* in Christ and *receiving* him. Believing in Christ means acknowledging that Jesus is the Son of God. But if that's as far as we go, it's like looking at an airplane from the outside and acknowledging that we believe it can fly. There's no personal investment in the belief. Receiving Christ means consciously accepting the free gift of his forgiveness of our sins. It's like getting on board the plane.

If you've never *received* Christ as your Savior, maybe right now is the time to do so. If you believe that Jesus is the Son of God, and if you would like to receive his forgiveness of your sins, I encourage you to do so with a simple prayer such as, *Jesus, I know that I need you. Thank you for dying for my sins and for offering me forgiveness and eternal life. I gratefully receive you as my Lord and Savior. I look forward to learning more about the purposes you have for my life. Amen.*

When I prayed a similar prayer, it marked the most important turning point in my life. I trust that it will for you as well. Money will not be the only area of your life influenced by your faith, but your faith in Christ will be the single greatest influence on your use of money.

Maybe you're in a different place. You've already committed your life to Christ and you've been walking the journey of faith for some time. But perhaps you're beginning to sense that you've wandered a bit by allowing our culture to get its hooks in you; you're looking to money and what it can buy for your identity or security. You gave God your heart, but you've been hanging on to your wallet. You have faith, but you also have a foot out the back door; you're covering your bases by putting an inordinate focus on accumulating money and things.

Maybe right now is the time for you to fully embrace your identity as a child of God who is fully loved no matter what you own, fully secure no matter how much money you have in the bank. You could do so with a simple prayer such as, *Jesus, I already received you as Lord of my life. Now I ask you to be Lord of my finances. I'm sorry for the ways I have looked to money and what it can buy to provide that which only you can provide. From this day forward, please help me look to you for the wisest use of the money you've entrusted to me. Amen.*

If you prayed either of the above prayers, congratulations. You just took the most important step in letting your relationship with Christ take precedence over your relationship with money.

Letting Faith Lead

The U.S. Open is one of the most prestigious golf tournaments in the world, and the golf course chosen for each year's tournament is among the most difficult. The fairways are narrow, the rough is deep, and the greens are lightning fast. It takes tremendous talent to win any professional golf tournament. To win a U.S. Open takes even more. A player must be at the very top of his game and his most mentally focused.

At the beginning of the last round of the 1996 U.S. Open, Tom Lehman held a one-shot lead over Steve Jones. Paired in the final group, Lehman walked up to Jones as they headed down the first fairway, and he did something remarkable: He prayed—out loud. Even more remarkable, his prayer was for not just himself but his competitor as well. Quoting from Joshua 1:9, he prayed that both he and Jones would be "strong and courageous" and that no matter what happened that day, no matter who won, God would be glorified.

Throughout the day, Lehman and Jones battled for the lead. By the sixteenth hole, Jones clung to a one-shot advantage, and as they walked toward their tee shots, Lehman did it again. Using the same verse he had quoted at the start of the day, he reminded Jones that "the Lord wants us to be strong and courageous." Smiling, he added, "That's the will of God."

Perhaps taking that encouragement to his own heart, Lehman rifled a bold second shot over a water hazard to the sixteenth green and then just missed his birdie putt. On the next hole, a par three, he almost hit the pin with his tee shot. But it was Jones who would prevail that day, winning by one shot over Lehman and Davis Love.[29]

Why would Lehman encourage the person he was trying to beat, especially in this most important of tournaments? Was it some ploy, some form of reverse psychology? Was it a sign of weakness? No. Lehman had a fierce determination to win, the same determination he used later that year to win the British Open and the season-ending Tour Championship and to finish the year as the leading money winner and PGA Tour Player of the Year. Through an unusual set of circumstances, I had a chance to meet Lehman, and I used the opportunity to ask him about his motivation that day. As he explained it, "I wanted us both to play to win, with courage and conviction, and I wanted us to be a good and faithful example of what Christians should be."

His encouragement of the person he was competing against was a natural expression of the faith that is the central part of his life, as it is for Jones. Lehman's identity and value do not depend on the added money, notoriety, or trophy that would have come with a first-place finish; they are based on his relationship with God.

So many of the financial problems people experience — whether heavy debt, little savings, or an endless cycle of purchases that don't satisfy — stem from the impatient and anxious strivings fostered by cultural messages telling us that this life is all there is and that our value and security are based on money and what it can buy. But that's settling for too little. We were intended to build our lives — financially and otherwise — on a foundation of faith. We were intended to find our value in and base our security on our relationship with Christ. Doing so frees us to use money in a way that puts us on the path toward home.

The Path Toward Home

There are only three things we can do with money: spend it, save it, or give it away. The *Builder*'s path is differentiated from the *Consumer*'s path by how those possibilities are prioritized.

Consumers make lifestyle spending their highest priority. A *Consumer* thinks, *I make 'X' amount of money, which means I can live in this neighborhood, drive this type of car, and wear this brand of clothing.* If there's anything left over after all that spending, a little something might be tucked into a savings or investment account for the future. In the unlikely event there's anything left after all that, maybe a little will be given away. This goes a long way toward explaining why people save so little, carry so much debt, and experience so much dissatisfaction.

Builders take the opposite approach: giving first, saving second, and then making lifestyle decisions such as how much home to buy, what sort of car to drive, and what brand of clothing to wear. It's an approach that leads to tangible financial success and lasting joy. The chapters ahead will help you get on this path and show you how to travel it well.

WHAT TO REMEMBER

1. Our most important true desire is our desire for relationship with God.

2. Putting God first in our lives frees us from looking to money and what it can buy for our identity, value, happiness, and security.

3. The Bible teaches us that when we place our faith in Christ, we become "a new creation." The old financial identity that has gone is the *Consumer* identity; the new financial identity that has come is our *Builder* identity. We were designed to use money for productive, God-glorifying purposes, such as building into the lives of other people and building lives of meaningful contribution.

WHAT TO DO

1. Review your goals once more. Spend some quiet time reflecting on and praying about them. Are these the goals God has placed on your heart, or are they goals promoted by our consumer culture? Will their pursuit or accomplishment be glorifying to God? Would you like to make any further changes? If so, go ahead and do so right now.

2. The Bible says that God views everyone who enters into a relationship with him as his "children" and that they are fully loved, fully secure, just as they are. In other words, our value in God's eyes is not dependent on what type of car we drive, where we live, or how much money we have in the bank. How might your financial habits change if you fully accepted the idea that you are completely loved, completely secure, just as you are? See if there's something you've felt the need to buy that you now realize you don't need to buy.

3. Do you really believe that God owns everything—your house, your furniture, and so on? One way to find out is to consider whether there is anything you would have a difficult time loaning to someone else. What would you have the hardest time letting go of and why? Write down some thoughts in your workbook on page 39. Begin looking at all of the things in your

life—your car, your clothes, your checkbook—and imagine that they all have tags on them that read, "Owned by God, to be enjoyed as gifts from God, to be used to glorify God."

WHAT THE WORD SAYS

Take on an entirely new way of life—a God-fashioned life, a life renewed from the inside and working itself into your conduct as God accurately reproduces his character in you. (Ephesians 4:24, MSG)

Part Three

How We'll Get There

Know where you are headed, and you will stay on solid ground.

—PROVERBS 4:26 (CEV)

I will set out and go back to my father.

—LUKE 15:18

Chapter 6

FINDING JOY: AN "IRRATIONAL" FINANCIAL ACT

Life's most urgent question is: What are you doing for others?

— MARTIN LUTHER KING JR.

It is more blessed to give than to receive.

— JESUS

Forbes magazine may seem an unlikely place for an article about charitable giving. After all, *Forbes* is all about business and making money. But there it was. Under the headline "Irrational Act," publisher Rich Karlgaard wrote not just about giving but about tithing, the biblical principle of giving 10 percent of one's income. He told about a friend — "educated and rational" — who earned a high income but could never save any of it. Raised in a strict church that required payment of the tithe in the same vein that the Internal Revenue Service requires payment of our taxes, his friend, not surprisingly, had drifted away from the church.

Now in middle age, with two degrees from prestigious universities and a thriving career, the friend found himself in church once more. There he heard another message about tithing. But this time it wasn't a finger-wagging lecture; it was a simple, compelling promise: Give 10 percent and you will be free from financial worry. That day, he and his wife decided to take the minister up on his challenge. "Almost immediately," Karlgaard wrote, "a mysterious transformation took place." Besides giving 10 percent of their income to charity, the couple found they were able to start saving 10 percent as well—they call it "the 10-10-80 rule": Give 10 percent, save 10 percent, and live on the rest.

Karlgaard also wrote about another friend who said tithing had helped turn down the "decibel level" of his life. "Every possession speaks to you," he explained. "Everything you own wants attention. When I began to tithe, I found a freedom from my possessions. I don't hold on to things as tightly anymore."[1]

At first glance, it makes no sense that giving money away could help us save money or experience a feeling of freedom. We all know that in order to save, we must first put money into our bank accounts, 401(k) plans, and individual retirement accounts (IRAs) and then see if there's anything left to give. And freedom? That's found in *more*, isn't it? Making and keeping more and more money.

It turns out that the people profiled in *Forbes* have discovered one of the most important of the many Bible-based financial principles: Giving money away benefits not only the recipients of our gifts but us as well, sometimes in very unexpected ways. Let's take a closer look at three reasons why the seemingly irrational act of generous giving makes so much sense: It honors God, it helps us make a difference in the world, and it provides us with great joy.

Honoring God

Many financial planners tell their clients this foundational piece of the conventional money-management wisdom: Pay yourself first. This advice is an outgrowth of the philosophy that life is all about us. The thinking goes, if we are to have enough money for our needs and wants, we must make savings our highest priority, putting aside a portion of every paycheck before spending any of it. While many people could certainly use some help on the savings front, I encourage you to *pay your purpose first.* We've already established that life is all about God. Therefore, our first financial priority is investing in God-honoring causes. The Bible refers to this as "firstfruits" giving.[2] The idea is to give from the first portion of our income, not from what may be left over after we've made the house payment, the car payment, and the cable television payment.

I realize that this topic can be somewhat uncomfortable, so let me ask an important question: Do you think God needs our money? I mean, is it possible that the Creator of heaven and earth and all the things in them could be running a bit short on cash this month?

Let's be clear about this: God doesn't instruct us to make giving our highest financial priority because he needs our money; it's because he passionately desires our hearts, and he knows that they get easily bound up in money. When Jesus said we "cannot serve both God and money,"[3] he was cautioning us that money would become his chief competitor for our hearts. Giving money to God-honoring causes is the most tangible financial expression that first and foremost our hearts belong to God. It's a constant reminder to ourselves that God is number one in our lives.

Making a Difference

While it's true that God does not *need* our money, investing in his work in the world gives us the opportunity to fulfill another of our true desires: to make a meaningful contribution with our lives. Here are three God-honoring causes where our money can make a difference.

1. Spreading the gospel. The Bible encourages us to tell others about God: "Go and make disciples of all nations, baptizing them in the name of the Father and of the Son and of the Holy Spirit, and teaching them to obey everything I have commanded you."[4]

2. Helping the poor. Throughout the Bible, God expresses his heart for the poor. Jesus even went so far as saying that when we serve the poor, it is as if we are serving him directly: "Whatever you did for one of the least of these brothers of mine, you did for me."[5]

3. Supporting those who teach God's Word. The Bible also teaches us to help meet the needs of our spiritual instructors: "Those who are taught the word of God should provide for their teachers, sharing all good things with them."[6]

So where do you put your money in order to invest in these purposes? If your church is involved in each of these, it is the natural starting place for your giving.

The local church is a primary conduit for the spread of the gospel, both in teaching attendees who are just beginning to explore matters of faith and also in supporting missionaries who are sharing the good news of Christ in other cities and countries. In many cases, the local church helps to meet the needs of the poor in their community, either directly by offering free food and clothing or indirectly by providing financial support to other ministries that work with the poor. And the local church is where we receive instruction in God's Word.

If your church is *not* directly involved in one of these purposes — perhaps it does not provide aid to the poor, for example — talk to your senior pastor to find out why. Because God's concern for the poor is so strong, if your church cannot or will not use some of its resources for this purpose, pray for God's guidance. You may end up deciding to split your giving between your church and one or more of the many excellent organizations that serve the poor. If so, I keep links to some of these organizations on the "Links" page within the "Resources" tab on my website at www.moneypurposejoy.com.

Now let's move on to the third reason why generous giving makes so much sense: It gives us great joy.

Deepening Our Joy

While our willingness to be financially generous demonstrates that God is our top priority, the Bible promises that we will be rewarded for our giving. Remarkably, we are even encouraged to *test God* on this one: "Bring the whole tithe into the storehouse, that there may be food in my house. '*Test me* in this,' says the LORD Almighty, 'and see if I will not throw open the floodgates of heaven and pour out so much blessing that you will not have room enough for it.'"[7] This is the only instance in the Bible where God says to test him.

Now, we need to be careful here. We are not to interpret these verses as a "Get rich quick" scheme, whereby throwing a few bucks into the offering plate will make a representative of Publishers Clearing House appear at our door carrying balloons and an oversized check. Our giving is never to be motivated by the hope for material gain; it is to be motivated by our gratitude for all that God has done for us.[8]

However, some people do receive material blessings that they trace to their giving. This is the case with my friend Michael. He was in the alley in back of his home one morning when he saw a homeless man picking through the garbage. Prompted by a message he heard in church the previous weekend, Michael struck up a conversation with the man. Then he offered him some money. As he reached into his pocket, Michael was dismayed to discover that all he had was a fifty-dollar bill. That was a lot more than he intended to give. But since he had already committed to giving the man some money, he gave it anyway. Clearly, it was a lot more than the man expected as well, because when he saw how much money it was, he cried.

Later that morning, Michael was at a building supply store purchasing materials for some renovation work he was doing. As he waited in a long line, a store employee approached him and unexpectedly gave him a certificate for 10 percent off his purchase. Michael was the only one in the line to receive a certificate. When the cashier rang up his purchase, Michael was stunned: The 10 percent savings covered all but $1 of what he had given away that morning. Now *he* was the one with tears in his eyes. Out of the many customers in line, why was he the one given a discount? Why would he get back almost exactly what he had given away that morning? He doesn't know for sure, but all he could think of was that maybe it was God's way of expressing his pleasure at seeing Michael's kindness toward the man in the alley and encouraging him to continue down the path of financial generosity.

The blessings of giving come in many different forms. But everyone I know who is generous with money receives a healthy dose of joy as a result.

To be sure, there's something hardwired within us that makes us want to hang on tightly to all that we have. But there's something else hardwired within us that makes us actually want to let go. I remember a time when our son Jonathan was about two and we had some friends staying with us who have a child around his age. As they played together, for much of the time they did just fine. But every now and then the word *mine!* would ring out throughout the house as they each pulled at the same toy with dogged determination to take it from the other. With a little parental intervention, one would soon let go. A couple of times — not every time, but a couple of times — I noticed that not only would the one who received the toy become happier but the one who let go would become noticeably happier as well.

The Bible tells us we were made in God's image,[9] and generosity is at the heart of who God is. He gave us life itself. He gave us his Son. Because we were made in his image, generosity is part of who we are as well. When we don't give or give only token amounts, we resist our nature and deprive ourselves of one of life's greatest joys. When we give, we live in harmony with our design. That's why being generous provides us with so much pleasure.

The connection between generosity and happiness is not just anecdotal. Social psychologist David Myers cites an experiment in which more than two hundred students were asked to make a list of ten people they knew best and then indicate whether each person seemed happy or not. Next, they were asked to go over their lists again, this time indicating whether the person seemed selfish or unselfish. The result: 70 percent of those judged unselfish seemed happy; 95 percent of those judged selfish seemed unhappy.

Myers explains, "Doing good makes us feel good. Altruism enhances our self-esteem. It gets our eyes off ourselves."[10] Of course, those findings simply confirm what Jesus said: "It is more blessed to give than to receive."[11]

For many of us, giving is a journey. That is certainly true of my friend Craig.

Craig's Story

Craig always found it difficult to give away money. He was raised in a community steeped in Christianity, but he doesn't remember ever hearing any teaching about giving. Plus, as an entrepreneur, he was accustomed to weighing the risks and potential returns of any investments he made, and it was always hard for him to understand the potential return from donating money. What held him back the most, though, was that money was always tight while he was growing up. Craig was just five years old when his dad left, leaving his mom to provide for him and his sister. How she did so without ever earning more than $25,000 a year still amazes Craig. His upbringing caused him to feel that no matter how much he earned and no matter how large his savings and investment accounts grew, it was never enough.

Slowly, things began to change. He says his wife, Laurie, has been "a huge influence." She always keeps a supply of McDonald's gift certificates with her and, as Craig puts it, "gives one to every homeless person she sees." It has driven him crazy on more than one occasion, but Laurie can't help it. Once, on her way to work, she saw a woman fall near a bus stop. Seeing no one coming to the woman's aid, Laurie stopped her car and got out to help. Even though she knew she'd be late for work, she insisted on taking the woman to a hospital, where doctors discovered she had broken her arm. Laurie stays in touch with the woman, checking on her health and sometimes even helping her buy groceries. Craig has gone with her several times.

Then Craig's mom died. It was a defining experience for him in many ways, including his journey with giving. He loved his mom. That was obvious by the moving tribute he gave during her memorial service. But he often thought of her as simply a hardworking, low-income single mom, not as a woman of significant influence. During a reception after the service, he was surprised at how many people talked about that very thing—his mom's influence. Some said her example made them better moms. Others said she influenced them to serve more or to be more forgiving.

Less than a month after the service, Craig talked to a good friend, Mark, who had been there. One week later, Mark had been to another memorial service, this time for an extremely successful businessman. Mark said that at the businessman's service, people talked about his business skills and career success. At Craig's mom's service, people talked about her generosity and kindness. During gatherings with friends or family, she was always the last one to eat. She wanted to make sure others were served first, even if that left her with table scraps. She was always quick with an offer to help, whether that meant making someone a meal or even mowing someone's lawn. Mark told Craig he had spent years looking up to the businessman, wanting to be like him. But now, more than business success, he wanted to leave a legacy of giving and service, like Craig's mom had. As Craig put it, "It turns out that my low-income mom was more of a hero than this millionaire." That conversation clarified something Craig knew deep down: "Life is about impacting other people."

At about the same time, the church Craig and his family were part of decided to buy a building. After twenty years in a rented space, the church would finally have its own building. When the senior pastor explained how various amounts of donated money would pay for a specific number of chairs or other parts of the building, it helped Craig understand his return on investment. As the pastor cast a vision for how the building could help the church serve the community, Craig felt excited about being part of it.

The night before the service in which church members were to turn in cards indicating how much they would commit to the building fund, Craig couldn't sleep. He wanted to give, but the amount that kept coming to mind seemed crazy. He spent the night agonizing over the decision, "wrestling with God." On the one side there was that familiar fear of not having enough. What if his business didn't keep growing? Shouldn't he keep the money in savings? Yet the figure kept coming to mind. He sensed God asking, "Are you really going to doubt that I'll take care of you?"

As night turned to day, Craig signed the card, committing to give more than he had made in a year for most of his working life. Laurie was on board with the idea of giving a sizeable gift, but she had no idea Craig would decide to give so much. When she saw the commitment card, she couldn't have been happier or more proud of Craig.

Since then, giving has been a lot easier for Craig. One day over lunch, as he reflected on his journey with giving, Craig said he sees his shift from amassing greater wealth to investing in God's work as putting his life more fully in God's hands: "I went from hedging my bets to professing my faith."

Getting Started

If you're not in the habit of giving money away, the prospect may not fill your heart with excitement. That's okay. It's not surprising, given our culture's emphasis on getting and keeping all that we can. While heart change is often the catalyst for behavior change, the Bible says it also works the other way around: "Where your treasure is, there your heart will be also."[12] In other words, our hearts will get involved *after* we get our money involved.

For instance, think about something you have a lot of money invested in. Maybe it's a particular stock. You probably check on the stock fairly often. Articles about the company catch your eye. Your heart is there because your money is there. Maybe you own a nice car. You think about it—a lot. You keep it super clean. Your heart is there because your treasure is there.

The same thing will happen when you start giving. You don't need to wait for your heart to well up with generous feelings before you start giving. Just take a deep breath and write that first charitable check. Don't worry, the Bible says, your heart will be right behind.

To get in the giving game, start with something, and then add more over time. Jesus condemned a coldhearted approach to following Old Testament laws about giving and other behaviors, as if checking off items on a to-do list. However, when asked about such rules and regulations, he didn't say to forget about them. In fact, he raised the bar, expanding the standard from letter-of-the-law outward behavior to spirit-of-the-law inner attitudes. Asked about the law against murder, for example, he warned against having anger in our hearts.[13]

The biblical standard of the tithe, or 10 percent of our income, remains a valid benchmark[14]—a place to move toward if we're not there already. By the same token, it was not intended to be a stopping point. In fact, every example of God-honoring financial generosity in the New Testament seems to go beyond the 10 percent threshold.[15]

Wherever you start, base your giving on a percentage of your income rather than an absolute dollar amount.[16] Work your way up to 10 percent, and then keep going. Your impact will grow and so will your joy.

Investing in Life Change

Early in the movie *Schindler's List*, war-profiteering businessman and Nazi party member Oskar Schindler boasts about the riches he anticipates making from a factory he buys with money coerced from Jewish prisoners.

> They won't soon forget the name Schindler here. I can tell you that. "Oskar Schindler," they'll say, "everybody remembers him. He did something extraordinary. He did something no one else did. He came here with nothing, a suitcase, and built a bankrupt company into a major manufactory. And left with a steamer trunk, two steamer trunks, full of money. All the riches of the world."

Schindler takes up residency in a luxurious home forcibly vacated by a wealthy Jewish family. Jewish workers do the hard factory work while a Jewish manager, Itzhak Stern, runs the operation. Schindler spends much of his time wining and dining Nazi leaders. He makes well more than two steamer trunks full of money.

But over time, as Schindler watches the daily horrors of innocent people being robbed, humiliated, and murdered for nothing other than being Jewish, something happens to his heart. He ends up using all of his money to save as many of his workers as he can.

When the war ends and Schindler prepares to leave the factory for the last time, one of his workers allows a gold-filled tooth to be pulled from his mouth with only a swig of alcohol to numb the pain. The gold is melted and turned into a ring—a gift to be given to Schindler as a sign of the workers' gratitude. They engrave the inside with a verse from the Talmud: "Whoever saves one life saves the world entire." Presented with the ring before he gets into his car, Schindler is overwhelmed with emotion, telling Stern he wishes he had done more.

"I could have got more out. I could have got more. I don't know. If I'd just . . . I could have got more."

"Oskar, there are eleven hundred people who are alive because of you. Look at them."

"If I'd made more money . . . I threw away so much money. You have no idea. If I'd just . . ."

"There will be generations because of what you did."

"I didn't do enough!"

"You did so much."

[*Schindler looks at his car.*] "This car. Goeth [a German commander] would have bought this car. Why did I keep the car? Ten people right there. Ten people. Ten more people."

[*Removing a Nazi pin from his lapel*] "This pin. Two people. This is gold. Two more people. He would have given me two for it, at least one. He would have given me one, one more. One more person. A person, Stern. For this. [*Sobbing*] I could have gotten one more person . . . and I didn't! And I . . . I didn't!"[17]

We don't need to look back on our past financial choices with the guilt that overwhelmed Schindler as he looked back on some of his. But we do need the awareness he had about the difference we can make with our money. And we need an awareness of the impact that our lifestyle decisions—how much to spend on food and furniture and such—can have on our ability to make that difference.

Sometimes we lose sight of the many needs that exist, or we feel so removed from them that they don't seem real. When an airplane with a hundred people crashes, it makes headlines. And it should; it's a tragedy. But because poverty is so persistent and so widespread, the need doesn't seem so urgent. Besides, we reason, what difference could our money make, anyway? Bill Gates' billions may help, we figure, but how much impact can our comparatively small donations really have?

But the needs *are* real. Incredibly, in a world where many people have much more than they need, many others still have far less than they need. According to the United Nations, a staggering fifty thousand people around the world die every day from poverty-related causes.[18] And our giving can make an impact. Just $7.50 is enough to provide a child threatened by famine with two meals a day for a month.[19] Even if our money impacts just one life through the sharing of the gospel or the provision of food, think of that. One *life*!

Equally important, our giving will make a tremendous difference in our own lives. Our hearts take a beating every day in our consumer culture. When we believe the lie that happiness can be ours if we just earn a little more money—always a little more—we settle for a life of chronic dissatisfaction. Fortunately, God has given us a way out. It's found in the "irrational" act of financial generosity.

WHAT TO REMEMBER

1. Giving money to God-honoring causes is the most tangible financial expression that, first and foremost, our hearts belong to God.
2. Through financial generosity, we have the privilege of investing in some of God's purposes, such as spreading the gospel, helping the poor, and providing for those who teach us God's Word.
3. Giving generously is one of the most joyful uses of money. When we are generous, we live in harmony with our design.

WHAT TO DO

1. Consider what, if anything, you sense God encouraging you to do about your giving.
2. Is there a goal related to giving that you'd like to add to your list? What is it? Write it down.

3. Read and meditate on 2 Corinthians 9:10-11. You may not think you can afford to give a full tithe or to give at all, but are you trusting God to supply you with enough to do so?

WHAT THE WORD SAYS

Excel in this grace of giving. (2 Corinthians 8:7)

Chapter 7

Expressing Hope: An Uncommon Financial Act

In the old days a man who saved money was a miser;
nowadays he's a wonder.

— AUTHOR UNKNOWN

Partway through the movie *The Shawshank Redemption*, prisoner Andy Dufresne makes an innocent comment to some fellow inmates about the power of hope. One of them, Red, doesn't take the comment well. He's been locked up a long time, and he's appeared before one too many parole boards that have no intention of releasing him. His response to Andy is angry and bitter: "Let me tell you something, my friend. Hope is a dangerous thing. Hope can drive a man insane."[1]

But Andy is all about hope. Wrongly convicted for the murder of his wife, his hope that the truth would one day come out sustains him. When the truth of his innocence finally does come out, a corrupt warden refuses to acknowledge it. Still, Andy clings to his hope for freedom. And he acts on that hope by chiseling an escape route a tiny bit at a time—for twenty years! Twenty years of hoping. Twenty years of chiseling. Twenty years of doing a little bit each day to achieve what he's hoping for.

Ideally, that's how saving money works. Motivated by our hope for a better future, we do a little bit each day to save for that future. Saving money can help us minimize financial stress, take a debt-free vacation, or buy a home. But if saving makes so much sense, why do we save so little?

At last count, at least eight organizations are studying Americans' attitudes and accomplishments related to savings, each with its own dire warnings. Among them:

- The Employee Benefit Research Institute (EBRI) found that over 60 percent of current workers have less than $50,000 saved for retirement. Even among workers closest to retirement, those 55 and older, nearly 60 percent have less than $100,000 saved. In a stark disconnect from reality, despite the low savings figures, 61 percent of workers surveyed by the EBRI feel "somewhat confident" (43 percent) or "very confident" (18 percent) that they will have "enough money to live comfortably throughout their retirement years."[2]
- A survey from the Consumer Federation of America and the Financial Planning Association found that 27 percent of Americans believe that the lottery offers their best chance for accumulating a $500,000 nest egg over their lifetime.[3]

In other words, most Americans are not saving enough; many are blissfully unaware of their need to save more, and some feel it's pointless to even try. With great regularity, new reports are issued, new warnings sounded, yet our savings habits do not improve.

Clearly, we don't need another research report, and we certainly don't need another lecture about our lack of savings. What we need is a compelling vision for the future. What we need is hope.

"The Best of Things"

Hope is one of the most powerful of all emotions. Hope for a better future motivates us to marry, go back to school, apply for a new job, and, yes, save for some future goal. If we are to do better at saving, we must do better at hoping.

The other night, I made our monthly contributions into the 529 college savings plans we have for both of our sons. I made the transactions online as I sat at a computer we have in our kitchen. Our seventeen-month-old, Andrew, was already in bed. Our three-year-old, Jonathan, was sitting at the kitchen table looking through a welcome bag he had received during his first week at preschool. With one child in diapers and another just starting preschool, it's hard to imagine our little guys as college freshmen. But we do imagine. And we hope. One of our hopes is that if they decide to go to college, money will not be an obstacle, so we're acting on that hope by putting money in savings month by month, a little at a time. By the time Andrew is old enough for college, we will have been chipping away at that goal for twenty years.

If you feel it's your duty to put money in a 401(k) plan or an IRA, chances are you won't. But if you have a God-honoring vision for your later years, something that fills you with hope, chances are better you'll succeed. If you feel *obligated* to put money away to help your kids pay for college, odds are it'll be a struggle. But if you're filled with hope that you will build a better future for them by helping them pay for college, chances are better you'll find the money.

At one point in *The Shawshank Redemption*, Andy says, "Hope is a good thing, maybe the best of things." I agree, as long as our financial hopes are based on our true desires to enhance our relationships, make a meaningful contribution with our lives, and honor God. This involves staying mindful of those desires, choosing financial goals that will help us fulfill them, and acting on them — all the while living in a culture that does its best to pull us off course.

Our consumer culture seems intent on discouraging us from saving money. "Buy Now!" the marketers' ads scream, with the implication that whatever they're selling will fulfill our hope for happiness. And with no-money-down, interest-only financing available, why *not* buy now? Why go through all the trouble of waiting and saving? But the hope hyped in television ads often turns out to be *false* hope. It's the type of hope that's "a dangerous thing" because it sets up the expectation of happiness while delivering only short-term pleasure and long-term financial pressure and stress. It's the "hope deferred" that the Bible says makes our hearts sick.[4]

The solution is to choose financial goals specifically designed to help fulfill our true desires. Doing so creates true hope, which makes us more likely to do what it takes to see such hope fulfilled, like patiently building savings. When we stretch too far to buy a home because of its bells and whistles that we believe will make us happy, we succumb to false hope. The bells and whistles won't make such sweet sounds when the mortgage payment starts to overwhelm us. But waiting a bit longer, until we can put enough down so that the monthly payment leaves us with financial margin, can make our hope for the very same home a true hope. In that context, knowing that the purchase will leave us with the wherewithal to give and save, the waiting and saving won't feel like a sacrifice. (We'll talk through more specific guidelines for buying homes in chapters 9 and 10.)

The If, When, and Why of Savings

Now let's get specific about translating our hopes into savings. I separate savings into three types: *If*, *When*, and *Why* savings. In chapter 9, I'll walk you through a process for calculating specific goals for each type of savings. For now we'll focus on the purpose of each type and where to keep such money (a chart on page 91 summarizes the points that follow).

If savings is for what could go wrong (if the roof starts to leak, if the car breaks down, and especially if you lose your job).

When savings enables you to properly maintain your possessions (when the car needs service), pay for gifts without going into debt (when Christmas arrives), be prepared for bills that come due less often than monthly (when the semiannual property tax bill or annual life insurance bill arrives), use cash instead of credit to replace your worn-out possessions (when the water heater develops a preference for cold water), save for goals to be accomplished within the next five to ten years (when you decide to buy a house), and work toward your more distant goals (when your kids head off to college or when you stop working for pay in your later years).

Why savings makes it possible for you to pursue a dream connected to your true desires (why you're here). Not everyone needs a *Why* account.

You may already be expressing your true desires in the course of normal life: the work you're already doing, the relationships you have, the volunteer work you do, or the time you spend with your family. None of these activities requires a distinct *Why* account.

It may be more exciting to save for a new car than a water heater, but each type of savings is important. When you have a solid savings base, you are free to pursue the goals that get your heart pumping. Without it, you risk taking one step forward only to take two steps back.

If Savings: Planning for the Unexpected

This is your emergency fund. In order to minimize financial stress and build a solid financial foundation, keep three to six months' worth of living expenses in such a fund. If you save even the minimum threshold of three months' worth of living expenses, you will be in an elite minority, as fewer than four in ten Americans have set aside this much in savings for the unexpected.[5] Most people are living on the edge, which means they have to take on debt and its accompanying stress if something goes wrong.

If money is not stock market or real estate money; it's money that has to be there if you need it, and it has to be easy to access. Put your *If* money into an interest-bearing but minimum-risk account, such as a bank or credit union savings account or money market account or a money market mutual fund. You'll get a better interest rate with a money market mutual fund; however, many require an opening balance of $1,000 or more. Also consider a savings account at one of the online banks, where rates tend to be relatively high and the minimum starting balance requirements relatively low.

You can't plan for all of life's ifs, but if you have three to six months' worth of living expenses in savings, you can cover a lot of them. Maintaining an adequate *If* account adds a palatable sense of peace to your life.

When Savings: Planning for the Expected

There are three types of *When* savings: near-term, mid-term, and long-term.

One purpose of near-term *When* savings is to cover the cost of maintaining your possessions. At regular intervals your car will need oil changes, tune-ups, and new tires. Your home will need painting, your furnace cleaning. Good rules of thumb are $75 per month per vehicle for maintenance and $100 per month for home maintenance, but it depends on the age and condition of your car and home.

Of course, you won't always spend the amount you have set aside. Those months, the money you allocated for maintenance will build up in your near-term *When* account. You'll be glad to have accumulated some near-term *When* money during those months when you need to spend more than the monthly allocation. Maintaining your possessions will make them last longer and save you money in the long run.

Near-term *When* savings is also for gifts, vacations, and anything else you spend money on every year but perhaps not every month. Most people don't plan for the gifts they buy throughout the year, even though most gift giving is for celebrations that occur on a predictable schedule, such as birthdays, anniversaries, and Christmas. In order to avoid busting your budget and going into debt for the gifts you buy, estimate how many gifts you'll be purchasing each year and set aside some *When* money to pay for them.

People often also fail to plan for vacations as well as bills that are paid less often than monthly, such as insurance or taxes. If you set aside money for all such items each month, you'll have the money when you need it. Near-term *When* savings is also for goals to be accomplished within five years—for example, replacing a car in three years.

Your checking account will be the most convenient place to save for near-term *When* items that you spend money on every month or two, such as gifts and the maintenance on your vehicles and home. You simply allocate money for each of these items in your *Monthly Cash Flow Plan* (a topic we'll cover in chapter 9) so that it doesn't get spent on something else.

For near-term *When* items that you spend money on less often, such as a semiannual property tax bill or an annual life insurance premium, put the money in a separate bank (traditional or online) or credit union savings or money market account each month. Set up an automatic monthly transfer of one-twelfth the annual cost of such items from your checking account to your savings account each month. With some savings accounts, you can pay bills directly through an online bill pay service. Or transfer the money back to checking when the bill comes due. For more expensive near-term *When* savings goals, such as the replacement of a car, use a money market mutual fund or a certificate of deposit (CD).

Mid-term *When* savings enables you to pay cash for things that will need to be replaced in five to ten years—perhaps an appliance or the roof on your house. This money is also for goals you'd like to accomplish within the next five to ten years, such as the down payment on a house.

Some people blend their *If* savings and mid-term *When* savings in the same account. Once they have six months' worth of living expenses in their *If* account, they keep adding to it, with the excess earmarked as mid-term *When* savings. But I recommend that you keep the two accounts separate. That way you'll be less tempted to use emergency-fund money for your next car.

A money market mutual fund, CD, or conservative mutual fund, such as a balanced fund, are all good choices for your mid-term *When* savings.

How much money you put in your mid-term *When* account each month depends on your situation. Give some thought to what may need replacing within the next five to ten years. How's the roof on your house? How old is your water heater? How long is your car likely to last?

Long-term *When* savings is for more distant goals, such as your later years, your kids' college tuition, or their weddings.

If you're eligible to participate in a tax-deferred retirement plan where you work (such as a 401(k), 403(b), or 457 plan), a life-cycle mutual fund within such a plan is a good option. With such funds, the investment style changes automatically, starting out aggressively and then becoming more conservative as you get older. Begin participating in such a plan once you have a good start on your *If* fund (more specifics in a minute). If you don't have access to a retirement plan at work, create your own with an IRA. If you are self-employed, consider a SEP-IRA.

If you have kids, an age-based mutual fund (works similarly to a life-cycle fund) within a 529 college savings plan is a good option for saving for college. (In chapter 9, you'll find help for estimating how much to save for college each month.)

I know a man who started saving for his daughter's wedding when she was just a little girl. Long before she ever met the man she would marry, her father was setting money aside for her special day, even when money was tight. Over the years, he could have spent more on himself, buying a better brand of clothing or indulging in more expensive cars. Instead, motivated by his love for his daughter, he built up a savings account earmarked for her wedding. When she eventually got married, the money her father saved was a great blessing to her. It was a great blessing to me as well since that man is my father-in-law!

By the way, I'm not crazy about the term *retirement* since it conjures up images of beach chairs and golf courses. I don't have anything against the beach, and, as you know by now, I'm not opposed to golfing. However, I prefer to think of retirement simply as "our later years." We might not do the work we're doing now (and then again we might), but we would be wise to plan on doing something more than building sand castles or practicing sand shots. With longer life spans, we may need the cash. Researchers are finding that it's also important to our health and happiness that we stay engaged in some type of meaningful work, whether for pay or as a volunteer.[6]

Why Savings: Planning for Your Dreams

Why savings relates to some of your greatest dreams. It was just such an account that enabled me to leave my corporate job to pursue the dream Jude and I shared of having me write and speak full-time about successful, joyful money management. Since we hoped to fulfill the dream within five years of when we started building our *Why* fund, we put this money in a money market mutual fund. However, if you'd like to build a *Why* fund and you won't need the money for more than five years, you may be able to generate a better return with a less conservative type of mutual fund, such as a balanced or stock-based index fund.

Is there something you're dreaming of doing? Maybe you'd like to take a year off and travel the world with your family, send your parents on a trip as a special anniversary present, or start a foundation. Putting money into a *Why* account each month can help you accomplish those dreams.

If, *When*, and *Why* Savings Chart

Type of Savings	Purpose	Place
If Savings	Emergencies (loss of job, excessive medical or car repair bills).	Bank (traditional or online) or credit union savings or money market account, or a money market mutual fund.
When Savings Near-Term	Intermittent expenses (home and car maintenance, gifts, vacations) and bills (insurance, taxes). Also for goals to be accomplished within five years.	Checking account for items you spend money on every month or two. Bank (traditional or online) or credit union savings or money market account for less frequent bills. Money market mutual fund or certificate of deposit (CD).
Mid-Term	Replacement of vehicles, home roof, water heater, and so on. Also for goals to be accomplished in five to ten years.	Money market mutual fund, CD, or balanced mutual fund.
Long-Term	Goals to be accomplished more than ten years into the future (later years, kids' college).	Life-cycle mutual fund within a 401(k), 403(b), or 457 plan or an IRA. For the self-employed, the same type of fund within a SEP-IRA. For college funding, an age-based mutual fund within a 529 plan.
Why Savings	Dreams tied to true desires.	Depends on length of time for the goal. For goals to be accomplished in less than five years, a money market mutual fund is a good option. For five-to-ten-year goals, a balanced mutual fund is a good option. For longer-term goals, stock-based index or life-cycle funds are good options.

When Plans Change

It's wise to set goals and plan for their accomplishment, but sometimes our goals change. Having money in savings gives you the flexibility to redirect it to a new goal that may be more important than the one you had in mind when you started saving. That's what happened to Bob and Jody. They had been saving money to replace their van. But just when it was reaching the end of its useful life, their plans changed.

For as long as she can remember, Jody felt called to motherhood and dreamed of being a mom. When she had difficulty conceiving, she thought her worst fears were being realized. Eventually, fertility treatments enabled Bob and Jody to have two children. Still, as Jody puts it, "I wasn't done mothering babies yet." Because they didn't want to go through fertility treatments again, their thoughts turned toward adoption. But their hearts' desire came with a hard financial reality: adoption fees of $12,000. Neither recalls ever thinking twice about their decision to put the money they had earmarked for a van toward the adoption fees. It was not a trade-off. A van was, well, just a van. Their decision to adopt a child was based on their longings for relationship and to make a difference in the life of a child who didn't have a family.

But what about their van? Didn't they need to replace it? As it turned out, their old one ended up lasting a bit longer than they thought it would, and shortly after they adopted their son, a relative unexpectedly gave them a van.

Jody and Bob's story demonstrates the remarkable benefits and unexpected blessings that can come from using money as an expression of our true desires. From the start of their marriage, they committed to giving a portion of all they received toward God-honoring causes as a way of acknowledging that everything they have is from God. They also committed to saving a portion of all they received and then living on what remained. For much of their marriage, Bob and Jody have lived on one income (Bob is a video producer for a nonprofit organization).

Throughout their lives, they've experienced some practical benefits from arranging their finances this way. For one thing, they haven't lived under the stress of debt; they have had no credit card debt, no vehicle debt, and they even paid off a fifteen-year home mortgage in about twelve years. To be sure, it has meant going without some of the things many people take for granted, such as cell phones and cable television. However, in return Bob and Jody have been able to experience something too few people experience: financial freedom. And here's something else they've experienced: God's faithful provision,[7] such as the unexpected gift of a van just when they needed one.

Getting in the Savings Game

So what do you need to do to build savings? Here are some practical steps.

Save at Least 10 Percent Each Month

As with giving, base the amount you save each month on a percentage of your income. Begin with the goal of setting aside at least 10 percent of your gross monthly income. You may need to save more, depending on your age, how much you have in savings already, whether you have children and want to help them pay for college, and other factors. If you're not saving anything, starting out at 10 percent may seem overwhelming, so start with a lesser amount. The key is to start.

Note that the 10 percent figure does not include near-term *When* savings for home or car maintenance, gifts, vacations, or bills such as real estate taxes or insurance premiums. Technically, those items are *expenses.* I refer to them as savings simply as a reminder to set aside money for such expenses.

Prioritize Your Savings

Here are some examples of how to prioritize your savings. Let's say you have an uncomplicated financial life. You're in your mid-thirties, you're single, and you earn $4,000 per month in gross income. You don't own a lot of expensive things that could break, as you rent an apartment and your car is in good shape. If you have little in the way of savings, each month put the $400 that you've allocated to savings (10 percent of your monthly gross income) into an *If* account until you have at least three months' worth of living expenses (I'll show you how to calculate your monthly living expenses in chapter 9). At the same time, be sure to allocate additional money each month for various near-term *When* needs, such as auto maintenance, gifts, and any nonmonthly bills.

After you have accumulated three months' worth of living expenses in your *If* account, you can reduce the monthly amount you're putting into it and start contributing to a long-term *When* account, such as a 401(k) plan. Let's say your employer offers a 100 percent match for every dollar you contribute up to 3 percent of your salary. Take full advantage of that by contributing $120 per month to the plan (3 percent of $4,000). That will leave you with $280 to continue putting into your *If* account. When you achieve six months' worth of living expenses in your *If* account, you could reallocate your savings by putting $200 a month into a mid-term *When* savings account (perhaps earmarked for your next car) and increasing your long-term *When* account savings [401(k)] to $200 per month.

Now let's say your situation is a bit more complex. You're married, you're in your forties, and you earn $5,000 every month. You have a thirty-year-old house, a ten-year-old daughter, and a five-year-old car. You have some money in savings but only enough to cover two months' worth of living expenses. Put 10 percent of your gross income ($500) each month into an *If* account until you have six months' worth of living expenses. At the same time, make sure you are setting additional money aside for your near-term *When* needs, such as auto and home maintenance, bills like property taxes and life insurance, and expenses like gifts or vacations.

Once you have six months' worth of living expenses in your *If* account, reallocate your savings, perhaps putting $200 per month into a mid-term *When* savings account for your next car or the replacement of your home's roof, while putting $300 per month into a long-term *When* account, such as a 401(k) plan.

You may want to help your daughter pay for college, but focus first on saving for your later years. You can get a loan for college if you absolutely need to, but it's tough to borrow money to live on in your later years. In the chapters ahead, we'll discuss ways to free up more money from your day-to-day spending, which should help you find ways to save for your later years *and* your daughter's college.

Make It Automatic

Opt for automatic deposits to make sure you never touch the money you've allocated to savings. If you're funding a 401(k) plan, your employer should be able to deduct the money from your paycheck and send it directly to the plan. You can do the same with a bank or credit union savings or money market account, a money market mutual fund, or other mutual funds in a brokerage account, such as those offered by Fidelity, Vanguard, and others.

Manage Your Raises

One good way to grow the percentage of income that you allocate to giving, saving, or accelerated debt repayment has to do with pay raises. Let's say you're earning $60,000 and you receive a 5 percent raise. That's another $3,000 per year. Unless you plan ahead, it's all too easy to absorb that extra income into lifestyle spending. If you're not at the 10 percent level in giving or saving, allocate a portion of your raise to each.

Robert and Sarah went even further in their management of pay raises. They've always given away at least 10 percent of their income, so for the first three years of their marriage, they gave away 10 percent of their raises and then took all the rest (after taxes) and put it into savings. Robert said, "I remember how taken aback I was when I did the math and realized what a significant savings base we could establish in just three years. All it would take was establishing and maintaining a reasonable budget, committing to staying within it for three years, and banking three years' worth of modest raises."

Initially, both Robert and Sarah had jobs outside the home. But they committed to living on one income, which made it easier for Sarah to leave her paid position after they had their first baby. The habit of living beneath their means enabled them to raise a family of seven children on Robert's teaching salary alone. They had no debts, except their mortgage, which they eventually paid off early.

Another way to start or add to a savings account is to sell some of that unused stuff sitting in your garage or basement. Many of us have things in storage that we're never going to use. Might as well sell it and put the money in savings. Income tax is another potential source of added cash flow that could be used to build savings. No, I'm not suggesting not paying your fair share. But, as we'll discuss in chapter 11, many people *overpay* their taxes. That money could be used for better purposes, such as building savings.

While many people could stand to do better in the savings department, some go overboard.

Too Much of a Good Thing

In chapter 3, I described *Stockpilers*, people who base their security on the size of their savings or investment accounts. Although it's wise to save, the Bible warns against the foolishness of hoarding.[8] Doing so can easily become an obsession that adds stress to your life and damages your relationships.

How do you know if you've crossed the line between saving and hoarding? This is not a black-and-white issue; there is no clearly marked line that puts you in the hoarder camp if you step over it. But there are some warning signs. Are you obsessively frugal, trying your best to spend the minimum in order to save as much as possible? I'm a big believer in managing our spending, a topic we'll explore in chapters 10 and 11. However, it's possible to go too far with this. Are you so intent on saving every last penny that when your spouse comes home from a shopping trip, you rifle through the receipts to see how much was spent? If so, you may be getting carried away in your pursuit of savings. One helpful step is to calculate a realistic amount that you're likely to need for your various goals and then agree to save no more than that. We'll walk through some examples in chapter 9.

One Day's Wages Out of Five

Twenty percent of your pretax income is now spoken for—10 percent for giving and 10 percent for saving. Does that sound like a lot? Does it sound impossible? Think of it this way: That's one day's wages out of five. It's not so unreasonable to devote half a day's wages per week to honoring God and making a difference in the world through generous giving, is it? And it's not so unreasonable to devote another half a day's wages per week to pursuing your hopes and dreams through saving, is it? That still leaves you with four days' wages to spend.

To be sure, traveling this path will take some proactive management of your expenses, especially with our culture encouraging you to spend five days' wages and then some on your lifestyle. It will also take traveling without the heavy baggage of consumer debt. That's where we'll turn our attention next.

WHAT TO REMEMBER

1. If we are to save more, we must hope more, tying our financial goals to one or more of our true desires.
2. There are three types of savings: *If, When,* and *Why* savings. *If* savings is our emergency fund. *When* savings is for home and car maintenance, bills and expenses that occur less frequently than monthly (real estate taxes, gifts), the replacement of our cars, our kids' college expenses, and our later years. *Why* savings is for dreams we have that are related to our true desires.
3. Set a goal of saving at least 10 percent of what you earn. That's just half a day's wages per week.

WHAT TO DO

1. Decide how many savings accounts you will maintain. I recommend at least one account for *If* savings, another for near-term *When* bills, another for mid-term *When* savings, and another for

long-term *When* savings.

2. Research the balance requirements and interest rates of several savings accounts. Start with the bank where you have a checking account. Chances are good that it will offer several types of savings accounts. Then look into an online bank, a credit union, and a money market mutual fund.

3. If you have three to six months' worth of living expenses in an *If* savings account, make sure you are saving for your later years. Does your employer offer a savings plan, such as a 401(k), 403(b), or 457 plan? If so, are you participating in it? If not, contact your human resources department to find out when you can join and then begin contributing a portion of your salary. If you are already participating, are you doing so at the highest level you can?

WHAT THE WORD SAYS

In the house of the wise are stores of choice food and oil, but a foolish man devours all he has. (Proverbs 21:20)

Chapter 8

Experiencing Freedom: A Brilliant Financial Act

If you think nobody cares if you're alive, try missing a couple of car payments.

— EARL WILSON

Note: Don't skip this chapter, even if you don't have consumer debt. It can still be helpful to you, as I'm sure there are people in your life who have such debt. It would be a tremendous gift to them if you could help them get out from under it.

I have a question for you. A very personal question. Do you have consumer debt? In other words, do you carry a balance on your credit cards? Are you making car or student loan payments? If so, what's the approximate total balance? My guess is that even your closest friends don't know the answer to that question. Yet if you have consumer debt, it is likely causing you some stress. Maybe even a lot of stress. And those bills are likely holding you back from pursuing your most important financial goals.

Consumer debt is like the proverbial monkey on our backs. It weighs us down. Our culture would have us believe that such debt is a fact of life, normal. However, having lived free of it for a long time now, I can tell you that it's a far better way to live. By getting this money monkey off your back, you'll be able to make much better time on your journey home, toward uncommon financial success and joy.

Woody Allen once quipped, "Money's better than poverty, if only for financial reasons." By the same token, living without consumer debt is better than living with consumer debt, if only for, well, lots and lots of reasons.

When you don't have any consumer debt, it makes things much easier financially, such as building savings. Just think about what you could do with the money if you didn't have to send those checks to your creditors every month. Being debt-free is also incredibly liberating emotionally. Imagine how you would feel if you didn't have any balances on your credit cards, if you didn't have to make payments on a vehicle loan, or if you were finally rid of your student loans. When I got out from under my $20,000 pile of credit card debt, a heavy weight lifted off my shoulders. I didn't realize just how much of an emotional burden my debt was (and believe me, I saw it as a burden) until I was out from under it.

It's also healthier to live without debt since stress can cause illness. It's even spiritually healthier to be debt-free. If you have consumer debt, you may find it hard to see the plan God has for you because you can't see past your bills. Living without consumer debt gives us tremendous flexibility. If God is calling us to a profession that pays less than our current job or perhaps to part-time work, we can actually entertain the thought.

If you have consumer debt, I have good news for you and what may sound like less-than-good news. First, the good news: It is indeed possible to get out from under that debt without declaring bankruptcy or winning the lottery. I'm living proof. And once you're out of debt, it's possible to stay out of it for the rest of your life. Now for what may sound like less-than-good news: Depending on how much debt you have, it may take some time. In my case, it took four and a half years to pay off my credit cards and another three years to wipe out my automobile debt.

In this chapter, I'll take you through a proven step-by-step plan for getting the money monkey off your back—for getting out of consumer debt and staying out forever. Take the steps as we go through the chapter, either with the forms provided here or in the debt chapter of the personal workbook. But first let's look at what the Bible says about debt.

The Word on Debt

The Bible does not explicitly teach us not to have debt. However, it warns that debt can enslave us: "The borrower is servant to the lender."[1] If you have consumer debt, you can probably relate to that. When I had $20,000 of credit card debt, I sure could.

Circus founder P. T. Barnum put his own spin on that proverb, saying, "Money is a terrible master but an excellent servant."[2] Money can be an excellent servant when we take advantage of compound interest — the process whereby invested money earns interest, and then that money makes more money, and that money makes even more money, and on and on. For example, if we save $100 per month for twenty years, we will have saved $24,000. But if we are able to earn 8 percent interest on that money, because that interest *compounds*, our $24,000 will have turned into nearly $60,000!

Now take that same power and make it work against us. What's that called? The common name is debt, but I call it a disaster. To give you a sense of how terrible a master money is when it's working against you, consider this: If you have $5,000 on a credit card charging 19 percent interest and you make the minimum payments — today often set at 4 percent of the balance or $10, whichever is greater — it will take you nearly thirteen years to pay it off. Even if you have a more favorable rate — say, 9 percent — it will still take nearly ten years to pay it off. At 19 percent interest, you will have paid a total of nearly $8,200 dollars to cover that $5,000 debt. At 9 percent, you will have paid a total of over $6,100.[3] It's much more helpful to have money working for you, not against you.

The Bible also says that debt must be repaid: "The wicked borrow and do not repay, but the righteous give generously."[4] Our culture often teaches us that the best route to happiness is the shortest route. If we have pain, let's stop it as soon as possible. If we have debt, let's wipe it out quickly, even if it means walking away from it through bankruptcy. If you have debt and you eventually pay it off, even if it takes years, having done so will give you tremendous satisfaction for the rest of your life.

Finally, debt can interfere with the biblical teaching that God will meet all of our needs.[5] A credit card gives us the godlike ability to buy anything we want anytime we want. That cheats the relationship God intended for us to have with him — one of patiently seeking his guidance, waiting on his timing, learning what he would have us learn in the waiting, and trusting in his provision. Maybe God plans to give us the very thing we're tempted to buy on credit, if we will just wait a little while. Or maybe he simply wants to strengthen our patience.

Preparing for the Plan

Our behavior around debt, like our other financial behaviors, begins on the inside. What we believe about debt, whether we're aware of our beliefs or not, influences our use of debt. Our culture has strong opinions about debt — namely, that it's expected and unavoidable. This message is screamed at us, "Buy now! Easy financing available!" and whispered to us, "You deserve this; go ahead and charge it."

Getting out of debt requires changes in behavior and attitudes. Both are important. All too often, those who quickly get out of debt eventually get right back in. That's because while their financial picture changed, their beliefs never did. Better to learn what caused your debt, including any attitudes that contributed to it. Then you can root them out.

Acknowledge the Causes of Your Debt

In order to help you understand what changes you may need to make, I need to ask you an important but sensitive question:

How did you get into debt?

Consider the following circumstances and check each one that contributed to your debt. Chances are good that more than just one factor contributed to your debt, so check off as many as apply.

- ☐ Unemployment
- ☐ Medical problems

☐ Divorce
☐ Small-business failure
☐ Living beyond my means
☐ Other _____

Did you include "living beyond my means" as one of the contributing factors? If so, I'm not surprised. That's what I often find. In most cases, to at least some degree, plain old overspending contributed to the problem. I'm also impressed. It takes honesty to acknowledge that. It's a healthy, powerful step to take personal ownership for your debt.

Now let's look at some attitudinal factors that may have contributed to your debt.

Confront Your Beliefs About Debt

I now see that when I was getting into debt, I believed nice clothes and expensive restaurant meals made me a valuable person. I overspent out of a weak sense of self-worth. A friend, Mitch, once had $75,000 of credit card debt. He did most of his overspending during periods of unemployment. However, he was using his credit cards not so much for necessities but in an effort to regain the sense of power he felt he had lost in not having a job title or an income.

Look at the attitudinal statements below and then check each one that applies to your situation. One of the best ways to root out a false belief is to meditate on the truth. After each of the statements, I included a Bible verse or two for that purpose.

☐ Everyone has credit card debt; it's normal, unavoidable, acceptable. (Proverbs 22:7; 1 Corinthians 7:23)
☐ Buying things makes me feel good about myself. My credit cards enable me to pick myself up when I'm not feeling so great. (Luke 12:15; 1 Samuel 16:7)
☐ Using my credit cards gives me a sense of power. (2 Corinthians 12:7-10)

What other beliefs contributed to your debt? Once you become aware of the attitudes that contributed to your debt, ask whether each one is true. Chances are good that they are not.

Consider Why You Want to Be Debt-Free

Now that you've assessed some of the factors that may have contributed to your debt, let me ask you one final question:

Why do you want to get out of debt?

What's your motivation? Think of the goals you developed in part 1 of this book. How much easier will it be to achieve those goals if you don't have any consumer debt? Write down any other financial goals you would like to accomplish once you are debt-free. Do your *If, When,* and *Why* savings accounts need shoring up? Would you like to save for a car or a down payment on a house? Keep these goals in mind as you go through the rest of this chapter. As you implement your plan for getting out of debt, being mindful of your goals will help motivate you to stay the course.

Now on to the plan.

How to Get Out of Consumer Debt and Stay Out Forever

What follows is a proven nine-step process for ridding yourself of consumer debt once and for all.

Step 1: Make a Commitment to Get Out of Debt

In 1961 when President John F. Kennedy committed to landing a man on the moon by the end of that decade and safely returning him to earth, the scientific knowledge of how to fulfill that commitment was not in place. The ducks weren't all lined up; scientists and engineers didn't know how they would accomplish the goal. Kennedy told the world of his commitment first, and then the ducks (and a lot of taxpayer dollars) lined up behind his commitment.

Scottish mountain climber W. H. Murray captured the essence of what it means to be committed:

Until one is committed there is hesitancy, the chance to draw back, always ineffectiveness. Concerning all acts of initiative (and creation), there is one elementary truth, the ignorance of which kills countless ideas and splendid plans: that the moment one definitely commits oneself, then Providence moves too. All sorts of things occur to help one that would never otherwise have occurred. A whole stream of events issues from decision, raising in one's favor all manner of unforeseen incidents and meetings and material assistance, which no man could have dreamt would have come his way. I have learned a deep respect for one of Goethe's couplets: "Whatever you can do, or dream you can, begin it. Boldness has genius, power, and magic in it!"[6]

Murray demonstrated great commitment in climbing some of the world's most difficult mountains and writing several now-classic books on the subject. He wrote *Mountaineering in Scotland* on a roll of toilet paper while in prison during World War II. He had been part of a British infantry regiment when he was taken prisoner. When his captors discovered the manuscript, they confiscated it. So he wrote the book again.

There is something powerful about making a commitment, as demonstrated by Murray's persistence in climbing mountains and in writing books under the most challenging circumstances. When our commitment arises out of a true desire to honor God, it is even more powerful. The Bible tells of a time when the apostles Peter and John healed a crippled man in Jesus' name, attracting a crowd of several thousand people, many of whom placed their faith in Christ. After spending a night in jail for causing such a disturbance, they gathered with friends to praise God: "Sovereign Lord," they said, "you made the heaven and the earth and the sea, and everything in them."[7] Why did they feel the need to tell God what he obviously already knew? Did they think God might have lost sight of who he is and what he has done? Not likely. Their words were a form of worship and a reminder to themselves that they were praying to the Creator of the universe! Perhaps we, too, need to be reminded of that as we consider the size of our commitments.

If you're feeling overwhelmed about your debt, take your frustration, discouragement, and doubt to God, keeping in mind the incomparable power of the One to whom you are praying. In the Good $ense ministry in which I have served for many years, we often talk about God's math—those unexpected ways in which he works and provides for us when we follow his lead. When people make the God-honoring commitment to get out of debt, I've seen countless examples of "events" and "unforeseen incidents" rising up in their favor.

Lisa's story is but one of many I know of how God provides. She once had nearly $10,000 of credit card debt. Soon after committing her life to Christ, Lisa found herself feeling "convicted" to get out of debt, so she found ways to proactively manage her spending in order to free up extra money to put toward her debt. During the process, she also wanted to begin tithing, so she made even more adjustments to her spending. Then she developed another goal: to buy a new armoire. Her furniture was showing its age, and she wanted a nice armoire to hold her television and CDs. She had a clear picture in mind of the perfect armoire, one with drawers to keep her CDs neatly stored away.

Shortly after starting to dream about a new armoire, Lisa learned that she was going to get a year-end bonus at work. The amount would enable her to buy just the armoire she wanted. She felt as though it were a reward for her commitment to get out of debt and start tithing. But then she mentioned the bonus to a friend who had been providing accountability and encouragement in her journey toward getting out of debt. Her friend pointed out that the bonus money could pay off Lisa's remaining debt. Lisa knew it was the right thing to do, but she was discouraged about not being able to get her new armoire.

A week or so after paying off her final debt, she was riding the elevator in her building with someone else who lived there. The woman was such a casual acquaintance that Lisa wasn't even sure she remembered her name correctly. In the course of the short ride to the second floor, where Lisa lived, the woman asked Lisa if she'd be interested in a free armoire. She had purchased a new television that didn't fit in her armoire. Stunned, Lisa went to see it and was even more surprised to see that it was exactly the type of armoire she had envisioned. Lisa said, "I felt as if God were telling me, 'I'm going to take care of you.'"

Are you committed to getting out of debt and never getting into debt again? If so, take a minute right now to fill in today's date and sign your name on the commitment form below. If you are married, you should both sign the form. (If you are using the personal workbook, sign the commitment form on page 60 of the workbook.) Don't commit out of a sense of pressure. Don't do it because I'm asking you to. Do it because, even if you can't see how it's going to happen, it's your heartfelt desire.

On this ____ day of _____ (month), _____ (year), I/we
commit myself/ourselves to going no further into debt, to doing
everything possible to get out and stay out of consumer debt, and
to praying regularly for God's guidance and encouragement.

Signed _____

Signed _____

Step 2: Go Public with Your Commitment

As Lisa's story illustrates, there is tremendous power in sharing our commitments with a trusted friend or relative, especially a commitment we're not certain we can fulfill. The Bible tells us, "Two people are better off than one, for they can help each other succeed. If one person falls, the other can reach out and help. But someone who falls alone is in real trouble."[8]

Think of two trusted friends or family members with whom you could share your commitment to getting out of debt. If you are married, count your spouse as one person you've gone public with, but each of you should choose another person as well who will hold you accountable. What does accountability look like? Simply asking about your progress on a regular basis, praying for you, and giving you words of encouragement along the way. Take a couple minutes right now to write in this box (or in your workbook on page 60) the names of two potential accountability partners—people you will ask to hold you accountable and encourage you in this process. If you're married, use the spaces to write the names of the additional person each of you will ask to be your accountability partner.

I/we will ask the following people to be my/our accountability partners in my/our journey toward getting and staying out of consumer debt.

_____   _____

Call your accountability partners today to tell them about your commitment and to ask for their help. Will you do that? Eventually, it would be helpful to share with your accountability partners your insights about what attitudes contributed to your debt so they can help you be on the lookout for those attitudes.

Step 3: Find Out Where You Are Right Now

In order to figure out how to reach your goal of becoming debt-free, you need to be clear about where you are. Some say, "I'm roughly $10,000 in debt." That won't do. You need to know *exactly* where you are, *exactly* how much you owe. You can get this information by filling in the payoff information in the *Debt Organizer* on page 112. Here's how a person I'll call Shari filled out her *Debt Organizer*. As you can see, she has balances on three credit cards and a car.

Debt Organizer

Creditor	Total Balance	Minimum Monthly Payment	Minimum Monthly Payment as % of Balance	Annual % Rate (APR)	Payoff with Declining Minimum Payments		Payoff with Fixed Payments	
					Months	Interest	Months	Interest
Visa	$1,800	$45	2.5%	18%	212	$2,315	62	$970
MasterCard	$500	$15	3%	10%	58	$123	40	$88
Sears	$1,200	$48	4%	9%	76	$247	28	$134
Vehicle Loan	$12,505	$396	N/A	7%	36	$1,356	36	$1,356
Totals	$16,005	$504	N/A	N/A	212*	$4,041	62*	$2,548

*These are not cumulative totals. Instead, they are the longest payoff period on the list.

To fill in the payoff information in the blank *Debt Organizer*, you'll need to gather your most recent credit card statements and vehicle and student loan contracts or payment books and then do the following:

1. In the first column, list each of your credit cards on which you carry a balance from month to month (not those that you pay off in full each month), vehicle loans, and education loans.
2. Fill in the total balances.
3. Fill in the minimum monthly payments required. For each credit card, use the minimum required payment listed on your most recent statement. For vehicle and student loans, your monthly payments are probably fixed.
4. Determine what percentage of the balance each of your credit cards requires as a minimum monthly payment. Just take the minimum monthly payment and divide it by the balance.
5. Fill in the "Annual Percentage Rate," or "APR."
6. Use an online calculator to fill out the four payoff columns. Go to www.bankrate.com, or check the "Resources" tab of my website at www.moneypurposejoy.com to see if any new debt calculators have been introduced. In the "Credit Cards" section of the bankrate.com website, you should find a calculator called "Paying the Minimum" or "True Cost of Paying Credit Card Minimums." By entering a few bits of information, you can determine how long it will take to pay off each credit card, student loan, or vehicle loan.
    a. First, it will ask for your current loan balance.
    b. Second, it will ask for the interest rate.
    c. Third, it will ask how the minimum payment is calculated. For credit card debts, just as you did in the *Debt Organizer*, take the minimum required payment and divide it by the total balance. Your answer will probably be somewhere between 2 percent and 4 percent. It will then fill in your minimum payment automatically. For vehicle or student loans, skip this step. Just accept whatever percentage is listed and let it fill

in a minimum payment.

   d.   Fourth, under "What Fixed Payment Could You Make Each Month?" enter the current minimum payment for credit cards. For vehicle and student loans, enter the fixed amount that you pay each month. Then click the "Fixed Payment" button.

   e.   Last, hit the "Calculate" button. It will tell you how many months it will take you to get out of debt if you fix your monthly payment on today's minimum. Then it will tell you how many months it will take you to get out of debt by making the declining minimum payment each month (the minimum required payment declines a little each month because your balance declines a little each month). It will also tell you the amount of interest you will pay. As you'll see, there's a big difference between fixing your monthly payment on today's minimum versus paying the declining minimum due each month.

Run this calculation for each of your debts and, using a pencil, fill in the payoff information in the *Debt Organizer* on the next page.

Step 4: Request Lower Rates

One study found that more than half of the people who called their credit card companies to request a lower interest rate were successful and received an average rate reduction of more than one-third.[9] So give it a try.

Once you get a customer service representative on the phone, ask to speak with a supervisor. Then say that you're calling to request a more favorable rate on your credit card. If you have received a preapproved offer in the mail for a card with a lower interest rate than the one you're calling about, mention that. Then ask whether he or she could lower your rate in order to keep you as a good customer.

If you were successful in negotiating a lower rate on any of your cards, fill in the new interest rate(s) and the new payoff details in your *Debt Organizer*. For example, let's say Shari negotiated to lower the rate on her Visa card from 18 percent to 14 percent. As you can see in the chart on page 114, this would reduce the time it will take her to pay off that

Debt Organizer

Creditor	Total Balance	Minimum Monthly Payment	Minimum Monthly Payment as % of Balance	Annual % Rate (APR)	Payoff with Declining Minimum Payments		Payoff with Fixed Payments	
					Months	Interest	Months	Interest
Totals								

debt by a whopping 45 months if she were making the declining minimum monthly payments, and it would reduce the amount she would pay in interest by nearly $950. Not bad for ten to fifteen minutes' worth of work!

Step 5: Fix Your Payments

Credit card companies are amazingly generous. As I already mentioned, if you make the minimum payments each month, they will ask you for *less* money in each successive month. For example, for Shari's $1,800 Visa, assuming a minimum payment based on 2.5 percent of the balance and a 14 percent APR, this month's minimum payment will be $45. However, next month's minimum required payment will be $44.40. Because the balance went down slightly, 2.5 percent on the lower balance is a bit less than it was the month before.

Of course, they haven't set up this system out of the kindness of their hearts. They set it up this way because if you accept their generosity and pay the declining minimum due each month, you will make interest payments to them forever! Well, not literally. But it'll sure seem that way. As you can see on the next page, if Shari makes just the minimum payment each month, it will take 167 months for her to pay off that debt. That's nearly fourteen years! And she will have paid $1,367 in interest charges.

Here's the simplest way to greatly accelerate the process of getting out of debt. Instead of making the declining minimum payment each month, keep paying the amount that's due this month. In other words, if this month's minimum is $45, keep paying that amount each month, even when your minimum payment due is $44.40 or $43.81 or $43.22. If you can afford $45 this month, chances are you can afford $45 next month. And if you fix your monthly payment at this month's minimum, you will get out of debt a lot faster. As shown in the chart on the next page, if Shari fixes all of her monthly payments, she will cut her interest payments nearly in half and erase her $16,000 debt in just 55 months. That's nine years faster than it would be if she made the declining minimum payments.

Debt Organizer

Creditor	Total Balance	Minimum Monthly Payment	Minimum Monthly Payment as % of Balance	Annual % Rate (APR)	Payoff with Declining Minimum Payments		Payoff with Fixed Payments	
					Months	Interest	Months	Interest
Visa	$1,800	$45	2.5%	14%	167	$1,367	55	$639
MasterCard	$500	$15	3%	10%	58	$123	40	$88
Sears	$1,200	$48	4%	9%	76	$247	28	$134
Vehicle Loan	$12,505	$396	N/A	7%	36	$1,356	36	$1,356
Totals	$16,005	$504	N/A	N/A	167	$3,093	55	$2,217

Step 6: Fix and *Roll*

If you have multiple debts, once you've paid off one of them, the money you were sending to that creditor each month can make a huge difference in how long it takes you to get completely out of consumer debt. If you're not intentional about it, the money will easily get absorbed into lifestyle spending. But there are better uses for that money, such as adding it to the amount you're using to pay off another debt.

This approach is a continuation of the philosophy, *If you can afford a certain payment this month, you can probably afford the same payment next month.* Just continue using the total amount you are devoting to debt repayment each month, even when a bill gets paid off. Take the money you were using for the bill that is now paid off and put it toward the next bill.

It's often the case that when you fix your monthly payments on today's minimums, the first debt to get paid off is the lowest-balance debt. But not always. In Shari's case, because the minimum required payment on her Sears bill is set at a relatively high 4 percent of the balance, and because the APR on that card is relatively low, that bill ends up getting paid off the quickest.

Once that bill is gone, where should she put the $48 she was sending to Sears each month? She should add it to what she's paying on the next-lowest-balance debt on her list, which is her MasterCard. Once that one is completely wiped out, she should take the full amount she was sending to MasterCard ($63) and add it to the payment for her next-lowest-balance debt: her Visa bill. When that one is wiped out, she should devote all of what she was sending to Visa ($108) and use it to accelerate payments on her car loan.

As you can see in the chart on the next page, by using this *fix and roll* process, Shari will be out of debt in thirty-six months instead of fifty-five, and she'll save a little over $100 on interest.

Step 7: Fix and *Accelerate* the Roll

One final step to getting out of debt even faster is to use an *accelerator*—a sum of money beyond today's required minimums. Even an extra $25

Debt Organizer

Creditor	Total Balance	Minimum Monthly Payment	Minimum Monthly Payment as % of Balance	Annual % Rate (APR)	Payoff with Fixed Payments		Payoff with Fix & Roll	
					Months	Interest	Months	Interest
Sears	$1,200	$48	4%	9%	28	$134	28	$134
MasterCard	$500	$15	3%	10%	40	$88	31	$82
Visa	$1,800	$45	2.5%	14%	55	$639	36	$544
Vehicle Loan	$12,505	$396	N/A	7%	36	$1,356	36	$1,356
Totals	$16,005	$504	N/A	N/A	55	$2,217	36	$2,116

will make a noticeable difference in getting you out of debt faster.

Let's say Shari can add an extra $50 to the $504 she's devoting to monthly debt payments. Which debt should get the extra $50? The one with the smallest balance. In Shari's case, that's her MasterCard bill. If she fixes her payment at $65 per month instead of $15, she'll have that debt wiped out in just eight months, as you can see in the chart on the next page. Next she should take that $65 and apply it to the next-lowest-balance debt: her Sears bill. If she keeps doing this, she will shave an additional three months from the process and reduce her interest expenses by nearly $300.[10]

You may be thinking, *This sounds great in theory, but how can I come up with an extra $50 per month to accelerate the payoff of my debts?* Think of it this way: $50 a month is the equivalent of finding less than $1.70 per day. Do you think you could find that amount of money each day to get out of debt as soon as possible and start pursuing the goals you're really excited about?

Bret and Becky decided to *super-accelerate* the payoff of their debts. They started their marriage with $110,000 in debt, not including mortgages Bret held on a condo and a three-flat. Becky brought $10,000 of credit card debt into the marriage; Bret brought $40,000 in credit card debt and a $60,000 home equity loan. When I met them during a break in a workshop I was leading, Becky had tears in her eyes. They had recently totaled up their debts, and the amount overwhelmed her. Plus, they disagreed over what to do about the debt.

Even though their initial conversations about money were stressful and upsetting, they committed to getting out of debt. They were able to wipe out the home equity debt by selling the condo at a healthy profit. Then, for the first year of their marriage, they lived in the smallest unit of the three-flat Bret had purchased before they got married, a nine-hundred-square-foot apartment. They also committed to living on Bret's base salary from a sales job and using any commissions he earned plus Becky's income as a nurse to pay off their credit card debts and build savings. One year after getting married, they had eliminated their credit card debts and had established a solid base of savings.

Debt Organizer

Creditor	Total Balance	Minimum Monthly Payment	Minimum Monthly Payment as % of Balance	Annual % Rate (APR)	Payoff with Fix & Roll*		Payoff with Accelerate the Roll	
					Months	Interest	Months	Interest
MasterCard	$500	$65	3%	10%	31	$82	8	$19
Sears	$1,200	$48	4%	9%	28	$134	17	$94
Visa	$1,800	$45	2.5%	14%	36	$544	26	$385
Vehicle Loan	$12,505	$396	N/A	7%	36	$1,356	33	$1,325
Totals	$16,005	$554	N/A	N/A	36	$2,116	33	$1,823

* Does not include the extra $50 accelerator.

Had they chosen to use both incomes for lifestyle expenses, they could have kept up with their minimum debt payments while living in a much larger home. But Bret knew that the debt was especially stressful to Becky. Plus, they both wanted to have children and have the financial flexibility that would enable her to stay home with their kids. So in order to build a strong financial foundation, they chose the short-term "pain" of a small home and a lot fewer nights on the town than they both had been accustomed to when they were single. Today they have four children, and Becky is able to be home with them full-time.

Freeing up money to accelerate debt repayment often comes down to this: *How serious are you?* If you want to get out of debt as quickly as possible, examine *all* of your expense areas—even those that seem *fixed*. That's what Mitch did when he decided to wipe out $75,000 of credit card debt. Realizing that his $1,200 rent payment was his biggest expense, he started looking for a less expensive place to live. For a short period of time, he even found a free place to stay. When that place was no longer available, he did something he at first hated the idea of doing: He moved in with a roommate. By living with roommates, he was able to keep his rent payments low, which put his debt repayment on the fast track. As an added bonus, one of his roommates ended up becoming a great friend. (In chapters 10 and 11, we'll talk about more ways to free up money from each of the major spending categories.)

Step 8: Stay the Course

I hope this chapter has shown you that you don't have to be in debt forever. And I hope you've been encouraged by seeing how much more quickly you can get out of debt just by fixing your payments on today's minimums. But I know that despite the appearance of light at the end of the tunnel, you may still feel discouraged about your bills. That's why it's helpful to look for the larger purpose for your debt.

When I first woke up to the reality of how much debt I had, I didn't want to get out of bed. Although moving home with my parents helped me out financially, it didn't do much for my spirits. Oh, my folks were supportive—incredibly so. But going from living on my own in an exciting big city to living in my parents' basement in the small town where I grew up was a painful shock to my system. Even when I began making enough money to pay my bills and live on my own again, I sometimes felt overwhelmed by my debt. It seemed like it was going to take forever to pay it all off.

Shortly after committing my life to Christ, I joined a Bible study. One night our leader asked us to turn to 2 Corinthians 12. After someone helped me find the passage in my Bible, I read the following words from the apostle Paul:

> To keep me from becoming conceited because of these surpassingly great revelations, there was given me a thorn in my flesh, a messenger of Satan, to torment me.[11]

Paul never specified what "thorn" he was talking about, but it was clearly a source of discouragement and pain for him. And I could surely relate. My debt felt like the nastiest of thorns that had been twisted into my flesh.

> Three times I pleaded with the Lord to take it away from me.[12]

Boy, could I relate to that. I wanted more than anything for my debt to just disappear. Three times? How about a gazillion times?

> But he said to me, "My grace is sufficient for you, for my power is made perfect in weakness." Therefore I will boast all the more gladly about my weaknesses, so that Christ's power may rest on me. That is why, for Christ's sake, I delight in weaknesses, in insults, in hardships, in persecutions, in difficulties. For when I am weak, then I am strong.[13]

Those words had a powerful impact on me. While God had already used the pain of my financial mess to bring me into a relationship with him, I began to see an additional purpose for the long process of getting out of debt. I saw that my feelings of frustration and weakness were drawing me closer to God. He was using the experience to teach me patience, perseverance, and trust in his provision rather than trust in my own understanding. He was using it to build my character.

Don't let your journey out of debt be only about the money; let it be about turning toward home and expressing who you were created to be. Look to see how God is using the process to further develop your character, strengthen your faith, and help you be an encouragement to others. When you become debt-free, and even as you're in the process, you'll be able to help friends or family members who are struggling with debt. If you are willing to tell others beyond your accountability and encouragement partners what you are doing, don't be surprised if you find some who'd like to join you on your journey.

Step 9: Never Forget Who You Are: A *Builder*

A couple times in this chapter, I've mentioned Mitch, who once had $75,000 of credit card debt. His overspending occurred not only during periods of unemployment but also during an era of his life when he had "wandered away" from God. Mitch began moving back toward financial solvency after he began moving back toward God.

During a retreat, he sensed God saying to him, "You need to stop basing your identity on money. I want you to get your identity from being a son of mine." Mitch saw that he had become trapped by the belief that if he just made more money, he wouldn't have financial problems. But he realized that he didn't have a financial problem so much as he had an identity problem. Something shifted for him during that retreat. "I didn't have to spend so much anymore." Free from the burden of maintaining his identity through his use of money, he became highly committed to getting out of debt. And he became free to act on that commitment. By the time he and Shelly got married, Mitch had whittled his debt down to $50,000. One year after getting married, they became debt-free.

Mitch now experiences financial freedom that goes well beyond being free of debt. He says, "I've learned something about contentment through this experience. I don't fear losing my job like I used to. I've experienced firsthand that I'll be okay with little and I'll be okay with more."

For *Builders*, people whose primary purpose is to glorify God and to build lives of meaningful relationships and meaningful contribution, consumer debt makes no sense at all. Embracing our identity as *Builders* is the single most important factor in staying out of consumer debt forever.

Final Instructions

Unexpected expenses happen to all of us, so before you start accelerating your debt payments, make sure you have at least one month's worth of living expenses in an *If* account. Go ahead and fix your monthly payments on today's minimum required payments, but don't add an accelerator to the payments until you have at least this small base of savings. Having some money set aside for emergencies frees you up to start going after your debts without taking a step backward every time a surprise expense pops up.

One question I am asked fairly frequently has to do with tithing while getting out of debt. Specifically, is it okay not to tithe while accelerating debt repayment? Ultimately, that decision is between you and God. I've known people who have maintained the tithe throughout their process of getting out of debt. I've known others who have felt the freedom to give less in order to get out of debt as quickly as possible. I am not encouraging you to give less; I *am* encouraging you to pray about the decision and be honest with yourself. There may be other steps you can take to get out of debt without using tithe money, such as going from a two-car household to a one-car household, going without cable television, selling other possessions, living with a roommate (as Mitch did), or temporarily taking on an additional part-time job. If you decide to reduce your giving while working your way out of debt, give at least something every month — an amount that still represents a "firstfruits" gift, a choice gift. Don't miss out on the joy of generous giving.

Start Today

This process works. It's not a magic wand; it won't get you out of debt overnight. But if you follow each step in this process, you *will* get out and stay out of consumer debt. So why not get started right away by signing the commitment form?

Living without consumer debt is a radical way to live; in our culture, it's extremely rare. So is managing money successfully and joyfully. I encourage you to live radically.

WHAT TO REMEMBER

1. Living without consumer debt (no credit card balances carried from month to month, no vehicle debt, and no student loan debt) provides tremendous freedom, flexibility, and peace of mind.
2. If you have consumer debt, it is possible to get out of that debt and stay out of it forever.
3. Getting and staying out of debt requires changes in behavior and attitudes.

WHAT TO DO

1. If you have consumer debt, the two most important steps toward getting out from under it are to make a commitment (sign the form) and line up two encouragement and accountability partners. Call them today.
2. Begin to work the plan by committing to continue paying this month's minimum payment (or more) on each of your credit cards, even when the credit card companies begin asking for less each month.
3. Before accelerating your debt payments, build an emergency fund of at least one month's worth of living expenses.

WHAT THE WORD SAYS

The borrower is servant to the lender. (Proverbs 22:7)

Part Four

Help for the Journey

I have shown you the way that makes sense; I have guided you along the right path. Your road won't be blocked, and you won't stumble when you run.

— PROVERBS 4:11-12 (CEV)

He got up and went to his father.

— LUKE 15:20

Chapter 9

Navigating with a Financial GPS

Make no little plans.

— DANIEL H. BURNHAM

If a budget were a person, who would it be? I often ask the people attending my seminars that question. Answers have included: Scrooge, the Grinch, Darth Vader, and even the Devil. One person said, "My mother-in-law," and I didn't get the impression he meant that as a favorable association. The person who comes to my mind is Rodney Dangerfield. Rodney never got any respect, and neither do budgets.

Clearly, budgets have an image problem. Recently, I worked with the market research company Quester to conduct a series of online interviews, asking people about their use and impressions of a budget. Non-budgeters described the tool as constraining, restrictive, and rigid. One said that with a budget, "you have to think before you buy." Well, let's not do *that*!

Non-budgeters have lots of company when it comes to their resistance to budgeting. A national study I commissioned from the market research firm Synovate found that less than half of all households use a budget to guide their spending, and just 13 percent use a detailed plan.[1]

Most people seem to think a budget is something people go on, like a diet. Or they think it's for people who need one. They are wrong. In *The Millionaire Next Door*, authors Thomas Stanley and William Danko point out that over half of all millionaires use a budget to plan their spending.

They call it one of the essential keys to financial success: "Operating a household without a budget is akin to operating a business without a plan, without goals, and without direction."[2]

Uncommon Tool, Uncommon Success

The words *millionaire* and *budget* don't seem to go together, do they? That's because, as Stanley and Danko write, "the press loves to tout freaks of both nature and economics."[3] Television programs and magazines celebrate the lifestyles of the rich and famous: designer dresses; lavish second, third, and fourth homes; and cars that cost more than most people's homes. They ignore the non-celebrity wealthy who make up the majority of millionaires, people who are more likely to be found clipping coupons on a Sunday night than sipping champagne. It's just not very exciting to read stories about millionaires doing such decidedly dowdy things as using a budget to determine how to allocate their money. Stanley and Danko write this about Mrs. Rule, a composite of the many millionaires they've studied:

> Who wants to see her sitting at the kitchen table three nights in a row, putting together her family's annual budget? Is there anything exciting about computing and accounting for each dollar spent last year? Would you be thrilled to watch Mrs. Rule compute and allocate future dollars of income into dozens of consumption categories? How long could you stand to watch her carefully complete her annual allocations calendar? Well, it's not fun for Mrs. Rule, either. But in Mrs. Rule's mind there are worse things, such as never being able to retire and never being financially independent.[4]

The financial habits of most financially successful people are surprisingly simple: They live beneath their means, set aside a portion of income for saving and investing, and, yes, use a household budget to plan and control spending. Maybe more people would adopt such simple paths to wise money management if the year's best (or most beautiful?) budget-ers were featured on the cover of *People* magazine. Maybe the makers of budget software programs need celebrity endorsers.

More, or Less?

Using a budget is not about spending less. It's about spending *more* effectively so that we have *more* money for what matters most.

When we identify financial goals we're excited about — whether getting out of debt or buying a house — it inspires us to find the money to accomplish those goals. A budget is a financial GPS that guides our spending down the path of our highest priorities. For some people, a budget even gives them the freedom to spend more money.

This was the case for Sheila. When she married Mike, she was accustomed to living beneath her means. Even with a relatively low salary, she never worried about not having enough. She always had money in the bank. Because she grew up as one of five kids with a stay-at-home mom and schoolteacher dad, frugality is part of who she is. However, the money she had in the bank did not give her a sense of financial freedom. She allowed herself to buy only whatever would get the job done at the lowest possible cost.

When she and Mike got married, he had been accustomed to using a simple spreadsheet to guide his spending. As they used it to guide their joint finances, Sheila began to see that her standard response to any spending opportunity — "We can't afford it" — was based on an unwarranted fear that they really *couldn't* afford it. Seeing on paper that, yes, in fact, they *could* afford it — whether a restaurant meal or a better brand of clothing — gave her a sense of freedom around money she had never experienced before.

If you've never used a budget before, give it a try. I'm confident you'll find that a budget is not constraining or restrictive; it's actually incredibly freeing. I believe it's the single most powerful, practical tool for successful, joyful money management.

Using a Budget

Here's what you need to know to get started. Using a budget involves four key activities: estimating current spending, planning future spending, tracking actual spending, and reviewing actual versus planned spending. Let's take a look at each of these.

1. Estimating Current Spending

To get started with the estimating phase, make your own copies of the *Monthly Cash Flow Plan* (page 132) and the *Monthly Cash Flow Tracker* (pages 140–141). (You'll find full-sized versions of these forms in the corresponding chapter of the personal workbook. They are also available as a free download at www.moneypurposejoy.com.)

Fill out the "Now" column of your *Monthly Cash Flow Plan* as best you can. You may have no idea how much you're spending on groceries or entertainment or in some other category. That's okay. For now, take an educated guess, using a pencil. This will give you a starting point.

Start by entering your household's monthly gross income (the amount before any deductions, such as taxes or retirement plan contributions). The first line in each section is for the total of the section. Next, enter your current monthly giving. In the "Saving/Investing" section, if you're currently setting aside a fixed amount of money each month for an emergency fund, enter that amount in the "If (emergency fund)" row.

Remember, I recommend treating expenses that occur less often than monthly as near-term *When* savings. For example, if you pay your life insurance premium once a year, save one-twelfth of the premium each month. However, on the *Monthly Cash Flow Plan*, I want you to enter those amounts by their real category names instead of in the "Saving/Investing" section. In other words, enter one-twelfth of your annual life insurance premium on the life insurance line. Think about any bills that you pay less often than monthly, such as real estate taxes or other insurance premiums, and enter one-twelfth of the annual amount in the appropriate places.

For other expenses that are not fixed every month — such as gifts, vacations, home maintenance, and car maintenance — estimate how much you spend on an annual basis and enter one-twelfth of those amounts where appropriate.

The only amount you should enter where it says "When (near-term)" is for goals you are saving toward that you are trying to accomplish within the next five years. For example, if you are saving for a down payment on a house that you'd like to purchase within five years, enter the monthly amount you are saving toward that goal.

If you're saving for a goal to be accomplished in the next five to ten years, enter the monthly amount in the "When (mid-term)" row. Remember, the "Now" column is for what you're currently doing. We'll get to what you *plan* to do in a minute. If you're saving for a goal to be accomplished in more than ten years, perhaps your retirement or your children's college education, enter the total monthly amount in the "When (long-term)" row. And if you're saving for some dream you have that doesn't relate to one of the other savings categories, enter the monthly amount in the "Why (dreams)" savings row.

Now, as best you can, go ahead and fill in the rest of the "Now" columns in the *Monthly Cash Flow Plan*. Even if you aren't tracking your spending, you'll know what to put in some of the categories because they are fixed. For others, such as utilities, you may be able to calculate the monthly average if you have your last twelve statements. If not, just make an estimate.

Be sure to fill in the last three lines: your total monthly income, total monthly expenses, and the difference between the two.

2. Planning Future Spending

Once you are done with the "Now" column of the *Monthly Cash Flow Plan*, it's time to fill in the "Goal" column.

- *Monthly income.* In most cases, your income goal will be the same as your current income — that is, unless you plan to try to increase your income in the year that this plan pertains to.
- *Giving.* Did you write down a goal pertaining to giving after reading chapter 6? If so, write your monthly giving goal in your

Monthly Cash Flow Plan

	Now	Goal		Now	Goal
Monthly Income	_____	_____	**Income Taxes**	_____	_____
Salary 1 (gross)	_____	_____	Federal	_____	_____
Salary 2 (gross)	_____	_____	State	_____	_____
Other	_____	_____	Social Security (FICA)	_____	_____
			Medicare	_____	_____
Giving	_____	_____	Other	_____	_____
Church	_____	_____			
Other	_____	_____	**Food**	_____	_____
			Clothing	_____	_____
Saving/Investing	_____	_____			
If (emergency fund)	_____	_____	**Household/Personal**	_____	_____
When (near-term)	_____	_____	Dry cleaning	_____	_____
When (mid-term)	_____	_____	Gifts	_____	_____
When (long-term)	_____	_____	Furniture/household	_____	_____
Why (dreams)	_____	_____	Cosmetics	_____	_____
			Barber/beauty	_____	_____
Consumer Debts	_____	_____	Allowances	_____	_____
Credit card	_____	_____	Education	_____	_____
Credit card	_____	_____			
Credit card	_____	_____	**Entertainment**	_____	_____
Vehicle	_____	_____	Restaurants/movies	_____	_____
Education	_____	_____	Cable/satellite TV	_____	_____
Other	_____	_____	Vacations	_____	_____
			Books/subscriptions	_____	_____
Housing	_____	_____	Health club/hobbies	_____	_____
Mortgage/rent	_____	_____	Pets	_____	_____
Real estate tax	_____	_____			
Insurance	_____	_____	**Health**	_____	_____
			Medical/dental insurance	_____	_____
Maintenance/Utilities	_____	_____	Prescriptions/co-pays	_____	_____
Maintenance	_____	_____	HSA/FSA	_____	_____
Electric	_____	_____	Disability insurance	_____	_____
Gas	_____	_____	Life insurance	_____	_____
Water	_____	_____			
Garbage	_____	_____	**Professional Services**	_____	_____
Home phone/Internet	_____	_____	Legal/accounting	_____	_____
Cell phone	_____	_____	Counseling	_____	_____
			Child care/babysitting	_____	_____
Transportation	_____	_____			
Gas	_____	_____	**Miscellaneous**	_____	_____
Maintenance	_____	_____			
Insurance	_____	_____	**Total Monthly Income**	_____	_____
Bus/train/parking/tolls	_____	_____	**Total Monthly Expenses**	_____	_____
License/fees	_____	_____	**Income Minus Expenses**	_____	_____

Monthly Cash Flow Plan. Aim for 10 percent of your monthly gross income. You may have no idea how you'll accomplish the goal, and that's okay. Just keep in mind the words from 2 Corinthians 9:11 (NLV): "God will give you enough so you can always give to others."

- *Saving/investing.* Here again, write down your monthly saving goals. Aim for saving or investing at least 10 percent of your monthly gross income. This does not include the amounts you allocated to near-term *When* savings elsewhere on your *Monthly Cash Flow Plan*, such as car or home maintenance, vacations, gifts, real estate taxes, and insurance premiums.

If you have little in the way of *If* savings, start there. Devote the full 10 percent to building that account. To figure out how much you need to accumulate in an *If* savings account, add up your estimated spending in each category where you would have to continue spending every month if you lost your job tomorrow. Some expenses may go away or at least decrease in that situation. For example, you may be able to minimize how much you spend on entertainment for a period of time. But other expenses, such as your mortgage and utilities, would continue in their full amounts. Add up the monthly expenses that would continue and multiply by three. This is the amount you need to have in an *If* account at a bare minimum (three months' worth). Multiply that figure by two to come up with the preferred amount (six months' worth) of *If* savings.

If you already have a base of *If* savings (the equivalent of at least three months' worth of living expenses if you don't have any dependents; six months' worth if you do), set some other saving goals, such as saving for your later years. Fidelity offers one of the easiest online calculators for estimating how much to save. Go to the Fidelity website, www.fidelity.com, and search for "myPlan Snapshot." By answering just five questions, you can get a ballpark assessment of your later years' financial needs and how much to save each month. Then you can work through a more detailed assessment that'll take about thirty minutes.

   If you'd like to help your kids pay for college, my favorite site for calculating their needs and how much you'll need to save is on the site www.savingforcollege.com. Just look for "World's Simplest College Calculator."

- *Consumer Debts.* In this section, the important step is to set an "accelerator" goal—that is, a monthly amount that you could add to your minimum monthly payments to accelerate the process of getting out of debt. Once you come up with a figure, add it to the monthly amount you're now paying on the lowest-balance debt in this section and put the new amount in the goal column. Then transfer the "Now" numbers from your other debts into the "Goal" column.

We will discuss all of the main spending categories in more depth in chapters 10 and 11, with specific ideas for spending more effectively in each category so you can free up money for your goals. For now, go ahead and set goals in each of the rest of the spending categories in a way that leaves you with a balanced *Monthly Cash Flow Plan.* All of your income should be allocated, so the last line, "Income Minus Expenses," should be zero. Transfer your spending goals to the "Goals" row at the top of the *Monthly Cash Flow Tracker* (see page 140).

Some Spending Guidelines
People often ask me how much they *should* spend in each category, so I've included some recommendations here. See the appendix for more detailed views of these guidelines.

Recommended Monthly Spending Guidelines

(Three-Person Household)

Category	Percentage of Gross Monthly Income
Giving	10.0% +
Saving/Investing	10.0% - 15.0%
Consumer Debts	0%
Mortgage/Rent, Taxes, Insurance	25.0% - 24.5%
Maintenance/Utilities	6.0% - 4.2%
Transportation	8.5% - 3.6%
Income Taxes	9.6% - 16.6%
Food	14.0% - 5.0%
Clothing	1.9% - 3.5%
Other Household/Personal	2.0% - 2.8%
Entertainment	1.5% - 4.0%
Health	10.0% - 4.0%
Professional Services	1.0% - 3.2%
Miscellaneous	0.5% - 0.6%
Discretionary	0% - 3.0%
Total	**100%**

This is not meant to be a one-size-fits-all plan, as there are lots of variables to consider, from different state income and real estate tax rates to personal preferences. Some people place a high value on vacations but don't care so much about clothing, and vice versa. Here are some of the key values, assumptions, and caveats that went into my recommended spending allocations:

- The total amount allocated needs to add up to no more than 100 percent of income. I hope this is one area where we can all agree.
- The guidelines are based on annual household incomes ranging from $30,000 to $150,000. The first figure in the range is my

recommended spending level for a household earning $30,000 per year; the second figure is my recommended spending level for a household earning $150,000 per year.

- You'll see that in some cases the range *decreases*. For example, with "Maintenance/Utilities," the range starts at 6 percent and then decreases to 4.2 percent. At the lower end of the income spectrum, such costs will simply require a higher percentage of income. At the higher end of the income spectrum, the lower percentage still allows for a much higher *absolute* amount of money to be spent (due to an assumed larger home), but such costs should require a lower *percentage of income.*

- The guidelines are based on a family of three. If you have a larger family, you'll probably need to spend more on categories such as food and clothing, which, of course, means you will need to spend less on something else. If you are single, you should be able to spend less on those categories. (The workbook contains recommended spending guidelines for other-sized households.)

- I placed a high value on generosity, starting the giving allocation at 10 percent of gross income, even at the lowest income level.

- In the appendix, you'll see that beginning at the $120,000 income level, I show money in a "discretionary" category. I suggest using this money for additional giving as a first priority. As I said in chapter 6, the New Testament raises the bar in the area of giving, with every positive example of giving going beyond 10 percent. I am also motivated by Jesus' words: "From everyone who has been given much, much will be demanded; and from the one who has been entrusted with much, much more will be asked."[5]

- I placed a high value on saving, with 10 percent of gross income going to savings, even at the lowest income levels. Starting at the $75,000 income level, you'll see that I began increasing the percentage, eventually capping it at 15 percent. Unless you are starting to save late in life, will need to provide for more than your immediate family in your later years, or have many children you would like to help with college expenses, you should not need to save more than the recommended amounts.

- At the $30,000 household income level, I assumed that the family is renting and that it owns one car. At all other income levels, I assumed home ownership and two cars.

- I allocated lower amounts than are the cultural norm for housing, capping the percentage of monthly gross income devoted to the combination of your mortgage or rent, property taxes (if you own your home), and insurance at 25 percent, and then slightly decreasing that percentage starting at the $90,000 household income level. (I'll explain more about my philosophy on how much to spend on a home in the next chapter.)

- This is an *ideal* plan, meaning it assumes no credit card, vehicle, or education debt. If you have such debt, you will need to spend less in other categories in order to allow for those debt payments. I recommend looking first to discretionary spending categories, such as clothing and entertainment. Other categories to consider are housing (is a roommate an option?), transportation (can you get by with one car instead of two?), and savings.

- The last two points are extremely important. Keeping your housing costs manageable and living without consumer debt are the most beneficial, practical steps for being able to give generously and save adequately.

- I used the withholding calculator on the IRS website (www.irs .gov) to calculate federal income taxes. I based state income tax estimates on my home state of Illinois. Feel free to customize based on your state's income tax rate.

3. Tracking Actual Spending

Next, record your actual spending. As you spend money, keep your receipts in a handy place or jot down how much you spend in your day planner, PDA, or cell phone, or on a notepad. At the end of each day, enter your expenditures in the *Monthly Cash Flow Tracker*. Note that for simplification, the *Monthly Cash Flow Tracker* includes primarily just the major categories from the *Monthly Cash Flow Plan*, not all of the subcategories. (The workbook includes a more detailed version in the corresponding chapter.) You could also create your own tracker with an electronic spreadsheet; use one of the budget software programs, such as Quicken or Microsoft Money, or use an online budget program. But you really don't even need to go that far. In fact, most people who track their spending use paper forms such as the ones included in this book and the workbook.

Feel free to customize the categories. Some people find it easier to manage fewer categories; others prefer more detail. Frank had been using a budget long before he and Joan got married, and he liked lots of detail. He broke down grocery store expenses by household cleaning supplies and food items. He had an expense category for office supplies like adhesive tape and another one for postage. However, Joan wasn't thrilled about using a budget in the first place. Naturally frugal, she didn't see the need. She especially didn't want to spend time dissecting grocery store receipts into further subcategories. So they met in the middle. They would use a budget, but they would take what Frank now acknowledges is "a less cumbersome approach" of combining some of the categories he had previously split out. As you work with your budget for a few months, you'll get a feel for how much detail is helpful to you and, if you're married, how much is good for your marriage!

There is also some latitude in choosing what expenses go in a given category. Is that pizza you ordered on Friday night "Entertainment" or "Groceries"? You can decide. If you're getting close to your spending limit on "Groceries" for the month but have some room in your "Entertainment" category, call it "Entertainment."

Keep your *Monthly Cash Flow Tracker* in a place where you'll see it every day — maybe on your kitchen table or your nightstand. That'll help you remember to record each day's expenses. At the bottom of the form is a row with the numbers 1 through 31, which represent the days of the month. After entering your spending for the day, put a line through the date as a way of remembering whether you recorded the day's spending.

4. Reviewing Actual Versus Planned Spending

At the end of each month, total your expenditures in each category. The first few months of tracking your expenditures will be for the purpose of making the "Now" column of your *Monthly Cash Flow Plan* as accurate as possible.

In future months, as you compare your *actual* spending with the goals you set for each category, you may find that some of the goals just aren't realistic, so you'll have to allow for more spending in those categories while adjusting other categories accordingly.

If you discover you're spending more than you're making each month, you have three options. You could:

1. Sell some possessions, which may enable you to pay down some debt.
2. Pick up an additional part-time job for a season to generate more income.
3. More proactively manage your spending. For most people, this option is the most viable. The next two chapters are devoted to helping you do just that.

Remember, the idea is to free up monthly cash flow so you have more for what really matters. It's not about becoming a cheapskate; it's about making choices so that you have the money to invest in your highest priorities. If our culture had its way, we'd be buying $5 tomatoes, wearing designer clothes, financing cars for eight years, and stretching to buy as much house as possible. That's a recipe for living with no margin and little joy. When you're clear about what's most important to you, you'll see that a budget is the essential tool for allocating money based on your priorities.

It's Easier Than You Think

If you're a first-time budgeter, you're in for some pleasant surprises. First, you'll find that keeping track of your expenses takes just a couple of minutes each day. You'll also discover that you have more money left over

Monthly Cash Flow Tracker

	Monthly Income	Giving	Saving/ Investing	Consumer Debts	Housing (Mort./Rent, Real Estate Tax, Ins.)	Home Maint./ Utilities	Transp.
Goals							
Total							
(Over)/ Under							
Last Month's YTD							
Total YTD							

1	2	3	4	5	6	7	8	9	10	11	12	13	14	15

Month _____

	Income Taxes	Food	Clothing	Household/Personal			Ent.	Health	Prof. Svcs.	Misc.
				Gifts	Beauty/ Barber	All Other				
Goals										
Total										
(Over)/ Under										
Last Month's YTD										
Total YTD										
16	17	18	19	20	21	22	23	24	25	26	27	28	29	30	31

at the end of each month than you did when you were spending money without a budget. There's something about writing down our expenditures that makes us spend less, especially on impulse items. It's a form of accountability that encourages us to think twice before spending, stopping us long enough to consider whether each purchase will support our highest priorities or hinder them.

You'll soon see a budget as quite the opposite of a ball and chain. As you buy groceries, instead of feeling anxious, wondering whether the amount you're spending may keep you from achieving some other goal, you'll feel free. You will know how much you can spend while pursuing your goals and enjoying financial margin. You'll see that budgets are about *more*—more knowledge so you can be more intentional about your spending and have more for what's most important to you. They're about traveling smoothly on the path toward home.

WHAT TO REMEMBER

1. A budget may not sound appealing, at least not at first, but it is the single most powerful, practical tool for successful, joyful money management.
2. Most wealthy people use a budget to guide their household's finances.
3. There are four key activities involved in using a budget: estimating, planning, tracking, and reviewing.

WHAT TO DO

1. Fill in the "Now" columns in the *Monthly Cash Flow Plan*.
2. Fill in the "Goal" columns in a way that gives you the monthly margin to begin pursuing some of your most important financial goals. You may not know how you'll be able to meet your goals. That's okay. In the next two chapters, we'll look at each of the major spending categories, discovering ways to free up money to put toward your goals.

3. Use the *Monthly Cash Flow Tracker* to begin recording your income and spending each day. Keep it someplace where you'll see it so you remember to enter the day's spending.

WHAT THE WORD SAYS

If you have not been trustworthy in handling worldly wealth, who will trust you with true riches? (Luke 16:11)

Chapter 10

Teaching Money to Dance: Part 1

Movement never lies. It is a barometer telling the state of the soul's weather.

— MARTHA GRAHAM

Think about the last time you went grocery shopping or took your car in for an oil change. How would you describe those experiences? The necessary chores of daily life? A bit of drudgery? I believe that the day-to-day movement of our money—whether buying food or investing in the care of our car—is something of a dance. When we're clear about what matters most and use our money accordingly, the movement of our money becomes a well-coordinated—beautiful, even—expression of who we are.

But this doesn't happen automatically. We have to be intentional about how we spend money. I call this *teaching money to dance* because spending well is about having money follow our lead, like a good dance partner. Too often, marketers lead and we struggle to figure out where to step next, allowing our culture to push or pull us into purchases that may damage the relationships we value most, hurt our finances, and prevent us from fulfilling our true desires. Moving to marketers' music is like trying to dance with two left feet.

In this chapter and the next, we'll look at some of the common categories of spending, examine the conventional wisdom about each one, and consider ways to make choices that enable us to pursue our most important goals. As we go through these ideas, remember that spending well is not about figuring out how little you can live on. Obsessing over saving a nickel on every can of soup you buy will only turn you into a miserable miser. Spending well is about seeing that you have a great deal of choice in how you use your money, and it's about spending in ways that give you the freedom to more fully and joyfully express what matters to you most of all.

The Two Most Important Spending Decisions

The Wall Street Journal recently explored why people save so little. What reasons do you think it singled out? Lack of motivation? Denial about the need? A penchant for big-screen televisions? All of those may indeed be factors, but the *Journal* fixed the blame primarily on our housing and transportation spending, two of the largest areas of spending for most people. Government figures show that while the portion of our spending devoted to many categories has fallen or remained flat over the years, our housing and transportation spending has grown. Together, these two categories now account for over half of an average household's spending—up from less than 41 percent in 1950.[1] Although homes and cars are more realistic options for most of us than tents and bikes are, we could definitely improve how we spend in these crucial categories.

Bricks and Mortar

I remember hearing a Garrison Keillor monologue in which he said something to the effect of, "When we're young we dream of being poets or painters. But the one thing guaranteed to slam us against the wall of reality, robbing our thoughts of all rhyming words and watercolor waterfronts, is a thirty-year mortgage. Get one of those and you'll find yourself chained to a 10-foot by 10-foot cubicle for the next thirty years." Okay, it's a bit cynical, but it made me laugh. The best jokes are those that make us see the craziness of some of the behavior we take for granted.

Owning a home is tightly bound up with the notion of the American dream, and I'm certainly not arguing against home ownership. The profit from the condo we bought in an up-and-coming neighborhood when Jude and I were first married helped us afford the home we live in today. But people's strong desire to own a home, combined with their low savings and the mortgage industry's aggressive marketing of creative financing plans, has led too many people to take on too much debt in buying a home.

The conventional wisdom about home buying can be summed up in one word: *stretch*. The mortgage and real estate industries promote the philosophy that bigger is better as if it's an absolute truth. We've embraced that philosophy all too willingly. Evidence that many people are buying more house than they should can be seen in the popularity of interest-only and nothing-down loans. Another popular type of mortgage is the Option ARM (Adjustable Rate Mortgage), which allows borrowers to vary how much they pay each month, including the option to make a minimum payment much like a credit card's minimum payment. Making a minimum payment on such a loan can make the loan balance *grow*. In some parts of the country, lenders are offering fifty-year mortgages. Will people carrying such mortgages ever own their homes, or will they just rent from the bank their entire lives?

The popularity of today's many alternatives to traditional thirty- or fifteen-year fixed-rate mortgages, along with the increasingly common practice of borrowing against the value of one's home, either through a home equity loan or cash-out refinancing, helps explain why more people than ever are carrying mortgages into their later years—a time when people traditionally could enjoy not having a mortgage payment (in 2004, over 32 percent of households headed by someone age 65 to 74 had a mortgage on their primary residence, up from less than 19 percent in 1992).[2]

Take a look around. Do you know people who are stressed because of their house payments? Are you? The conventional wisdom about home buying often leaves people living on the financial edge, stressed that their adjustable-rate mortgage may rise and wondering what will happen if one of the two incomes required to make the payments goes away.

Here are some ways to make better housing choices.

Reject the Conventional Wisdom

Historically, mortgage companies have written loans for which the monthly payment requires no more than 28 percent of a borrower's monthly gross income for the total of their mortgage, real estate taxes, and homeowners insurance. A loosening of that standard has led to mortgages that require a much higher percentage of borrowers' incomes.

However, I recommend that you devote *no more than 25 percent of your monthly gross income* to such expenses, preferably less. Let's look at the impact of opting for the lower percentage.

My approach would allow a family with annual income of $75,000 to spend $1,563 per month on their mortgage, taxes, and insurance (25 percent of their monthly gross income). That would enable them to take out a mortgage for approximately $215,000. Assuming a down payment of 20 percent, they could purchase a home costing up to $268,750. The principal and interest on a thirty-year, 6 percent fixed-rate mortgage for $215,000 would cost them about $1,288 per month. Adding in an estimated $64 per month for insurance and $211 per month for taxes brings the total to $1,563 per month.

Now let's compare this approach with the mortgage industry's standard approach. Stretching to 28 percent of monthly gross income would raise the home buyer's allowable monthly payment to $1,750, which would cover a mortgage of around $240,500. If they could make a down payment of 20 percent, the homebuyers would be encouraged to stretch and buy a house costing $300,625. With the many "creative financing" options on the mortgage market today, they would likely be counseled to set their sights even higher.

Of course, my approach involves a trade-off. In order to enjoy almost $200 of more margin per month, the family would have to opt for a less expensive home. That might mean fewer amenities or a different neighborhood. But wouldn't the freedom to live with financial margin be worth it?

The chart on the next page shows my recommendations about how much house can be afforded at various incomes. These recommendations are based on spending a maximum of 25 percent of gross monthly income on the combination of mortgage, property taxes, and insurance. A number of other assumptions had to be made as well. For property taxes, I used the national average of just under 1 percent of a home's value.[3] In some parts of the country, property taxes are higher; in others, they are lower. Insurance costs also vary. Of course, if you make a down payment higher than 20 percent of the purchase price, you'll be able to afford a more expensive home than what is shown on the chart and still keep your mortgage/taxes/insurance payment to no more than 25 percent of your gross monthly income.

Consider All of the Costs of Home Ownership

When considering the purchase of a home, be sure the down payment doesn't leave you without an emergency fund. After making the down payment, you still need at least three months' worth of living expenses in an emergency fund, preferably more. A lot can go wrong with a home, and without a safety net, you're left to rely on credit cards if you get hit with an unexpected expense.

Take into Account the Pull of the Neighborhood

When shopping for a home, many people take into account the size, amenities, and cost. They may also consider the home's access to good restaurants or parks. If they have children, they'll check on the quality of schools in the community. However, most people fail to take into account the impact the surroundings of their new neighborhood will have on many of their other financial decisions. Neighborhoods tend to be so homogeneous that marketers can reliably predict "how many credit cards you have, which appliances fill your kitchen, where you buy your clothes, and the magazines you read" solely based on where you live.[4]

While it's true that neighborhoods attract people who are similar to those living there, they also tend to further homogenize those who move in. Buy a home in a more expensive neighborhood than the one in which

Recommended Housing Guidelines

Annual Gross Income	$30,000*	$45,000	$60,000	$75,000	$90,000	$105,000	$120,000	$135,000	$150,000
Monthly Gross Income	$2,500	$3,750	$5,000	$6,250	$7,500	$8,750	$10,000	$11,250	$12,000
Home Purchase Price	$106,250	$160,000	$213,750	$268,750	$321,250	$375,000	$427,500	$480,000	$532,500
Total Mortgage (with 20% down payment)	$85,000	$128,000	$171,000	$215,000	$257,000	$300,000	$342,000	$384,000	$426,000
Monthly Mortgage Payment (6%)	$511	$769	$1,028	$1,288	$1,543	$1,797	$2,050	$2,303	$2,554
Insurance	$29	$42	$53	$64	$73	$80	$86	$91	$95
Taxes	$85	$127	$169	$211	$252	$293	$334	$374	$414
Total of Mortgage/Insurance/Taxes	$625	$938	$1,250	$1,563	$1,868	$2,170	$2,470	$2,768	$3,063
Percentage of Monthly Gross Income	25.0%	25.0%	25.0%	25.0%	24.9%	24.8%	24.7%	24.6%	24.5%

* At the $30,000 income level, a family would probably be better off renting. Without a real estate tax payment, that would enable them to spend nearly $600 per month on an apartment. Plus, they would reduce their risk of having to pay for potentially costly repairs to a home.

you currently live and, over time, you'll likely find yourself taking more-expensive vacations, driving more-expensive cars, and living a more-expensive lifestyle.

When Jude and I lived in our condo in a working-class neighborhood, we felt no pressure to keep up. We were never self-conscious about what we drove or what we wore. Now that we live in a more affluent neighborhood, I feel more pressure to keep up the appearance of our home and its landscaping (although right now the weeds are winning the battle). While I still drive a fifteen-year-old car, I'm more aware of its dents and scratches. In our old neighborhood, I never thought twice about it.

Our surroundings have a type of magnetic force that pulls on us. The more upward the pull—that is, the greater the gap between us and the people around us who have more than we have—the more powerful the force. Sometimes the force is so strong we can almost feel it. Other times it isn't so apparent, but it's still there, and it's working on us. It's less expensive to live where the upward pull isn't so strong.

Consider Making This Power Move

What if you are living in a house that you realize is costing you too much? The mortgage payment is so high that it's tough to give or save. And joy? What's *that*? If that's your situation, you could do something radical. You could move to a less-expensive home. I know, I know, it's a crazy thought. Changing where you live is not exactly as easy as changing dinner plans. However, housing is the single-largest expense for most people, so, out of all of your spending choices, this one has the greatest impact on how much margin you have to pursue those things that will bring you the greatest level of happiness: your true desires. It wasn't easy, but that is exactly what Carol and Tim finally decided to do.

When Carol first saw the house she and her husband eventually bought, she knew it was the home for them. She loved it and envisioned living there for the rest of their lives. Shortly after moving in, they learned she was pregnant with their first child. After their daughter was born, Carol wanted to stay home full-time, but they could not make the mortgage payment on just one income, so she resigned herself to keeping her job as a human resources director. Years passed. They had enough money for their mortgage but frustratingly little time for their daughter. The passage of time only left Carol and Tim *more* dependent on both incomes, as a stint of self-employment that Carol tried didn't work out and left them saddled with extra debt.

Five years after their daughter was born, they made the difficult decision to sell their home. Carol wanted to spend more time with their little girl, and she and Tim both wanted to get out of debt. Their choice to move to a less-expensive town nearby enabled them to pay off their non-mortgage debt and gain the monthly margin they needed in order for Carol to stay home. Selling the house they loved was far from easy. However, even though Carol says that full-time parenting is much more demanding than her most challenging work assignments, she and Tim both agree that they are much happier.

They've also experienced a benefit they never anticipated. Carol says that two aspects of their move deepened their relationship with God. First, the speed with which their home sold seemed miraculous. Even though many homes in their community were sitting on the market for over a year, theirs sold within a month and for nearly their full asking price. They took this as God's affirmation of their decision to sell. Second, they saw that they had unintentionally moved God out from the center of their lives. "Without realizing it, I think we were trying to fit into the culture," Carol explained. "Our identities were in where we lived and what we did. They weren't where they should be. When we made this move, it stripped away a lot of things for us. I think of it as kind of a time-out. It's been a reminder that we are just as treasured and just as worthy if we live here as if we lived somewhere else."

If you're spending too much on housing, moving to a less expensive home will powerfully and positively impact your monthly financial margin. Sure, others may raise their eyebrows as you take what, to them, looks like a step backward. But it won't be. It will be a bold expression of what truly matters to you. Your example may even cause others to rethink their own financial decisions, giving them the motivation to make the same courageous move.

Now let's see how you can improve your spending for what is typically the second-largest household expense.

Wheels

Our home may be our castle, but nearly half of all car owners see their car as a reflection of who they are.[5] The belief that we are what we drive, coupled with the auto industry's heavy use of planned obsolescence — the yearly rollout of new models with "must-have" new features — often leaves us overspending on what we drive. Consider the following:

- People tend to keep their vehicles about three years,[6] even though the average life span of a vehicle is twelve years.[7]
- The average vehicle loan now exceeds $24,700, and the average loan now stretches to over five years. Some banks are even writing vehicle loans for as long as nine years, making them seem more like mortgages.[8]
- Nearly 40 percent of new-car buyers owe more on their trade-in than it is worth.[9] People in that situation often roll the remainder of what they owe on their trade-in into their new loan, covering the added cost by choosing longer loans.

In other words, the conventional wisdom is to build short-term relationships with our vehicles and long-term relationships with our vehicles' loan officers.

Break the Financing Cycle

A better approach to buying cars is to do the opposite of what is customary. In this case, that means building long-term relationships with our vehicles and ending our relationship with our vehicles' loan officers. More specifically, I recommend keeping a car for at least ten years, preferably longer. The financial freedom this brings is far more beneficial than the short-lived thrill of driving a car with temperature-controlled cup holders. Here are some guidelines for how to break the cycle of financing cars.

1. Buy, don't lease. Although you may pay less each month for a leased car than you do for a car you buy and finance, you won't own anything at the end of the lease. You'll just have to start making payments on another vehicle. In order to grow your monthly margin, it helps a lot to have no monthly car payment.

2. If you're currently making payments on a car or truck loan, keep making payments even after your vehicle is paid off. Just send them to a savings account (your mid-term *When* account) instead of to your lender. If you can afford the payment today, you can afford it once the loan is paid off. The average monthly payment for a financed new car now tops $480.[10] If you saved that amount every month after your car loan is paid off—$5,760 a year—you'd have $17,280 at the end of three years, or $23,040 after four years, and that doesn't include interest earned from a money market mutual fund or the trade-in value of your current car. That will enable you to buy your next car with cash.

3. When it comes time to replace your current vehicle, opt for a well-maintained used car. Even vehicles used by dealers for test-drives or loaners will be less expensive than a brand-new car. But vehicles that are one to two years old are where the real deals can be found; they often cost 30 to 40 percent less than the original price.

4. When deciding which car to buy, consider all of the costs. Some cars are more expensive than others to insure and maintain. When the exhaust system goes out on a dual-exhaust car, for example, it's going to cost a lot more than it would on a car with a single-exhaust system. Edmunds.com has a helpful "True Cost to Own" calculator that enables you to compare vehicles based on the costs of fuel, insurance, maintenance, replacement parts, and depreciation. Call your insurance agent to get quotes on a few cars you're considering as a point of comparison to what the Edmunds website tells you. You can run a separate fuel economy comparison at www.fueleconomy.gov.

5. Lower your insurance bill. One of the financial perks of keeping a car a long time is that eventually you can reduce your insurance costs. No matter how old your car is, look into the cost savings of raising your deductibles. Before opting for a higher deductible, however, make sure you have enough money in your *If* account to cover it. At a certain point, you may want to drop collision and comprehensive (the latter covers fire, vandalism, and theft) coverage all together, keeping only liability coverage. That's what we did with our oldest car.

6. Consider how many vehicles you really need. We're so intent on having our own vehicle that the number of registered vehicles per household now exceeds the number of licensed drivers per household.[11] No wonder one-fifth of all new homes now come with three-car garages.[12]

When it comes to deciding which car to buy, think like a *Builder* rather than a *Consumer*. There are certainly no moral prohibitions against heated seats or headlight wipers. However, thinking like a *Builder* will enable you to reject a belief system that says you are what you drive. It will free you to choose a car that helps you live with financial margin. When you see ads for new models that can parallel park themselves, you can easily pass because you know that keeping your current car longer is part of a broader strategy to accomplish goals that are more important to you.

The Choice Is Yours

How you spend money matters greatly. While some of your bills appear to be fixed, you have a choice about how you allocate *all* of your resources. That's why I had the audacity to suggest changing houses if your mortgage payment is leaving you tripping over your financial feet.

In the next chapter, we'll continue to explore some of the common areas of spending. Remember, this is not tightwad training; this is about having our true desires "cut in" on our consumer culture. When we choose to keep a car for ten or more years in order to have the margin to save for our later years, we are not suffering; we are making our money dance to the tune of what matters most. Looked at that way, even seemingly routine spending choices can become powerful, joyful expressions of our true desires.

WHAT TO REMEMBER

1. Two of your most important financial decisions are how much to spend on housing and transportation.
2. Spend no more than 25 percent of your gross monthly income (preferably less) on the combination of your mortgage payment, real estate taxes, and insurance.
3. Break the cycle of financing vehicles and you will gain tremendous financial freedom.

WHAT TO DO

1. Figure out what percentage of your monthly gross income is going toward your mortgage/rent plus homeowners/renters insurance and real estate taxes (if you own).
2. If the percentage is higher than 25 percent, consider some remedies. If you rent, consider moving to a less expensive apartment or living with a roommate. If you own, as radical as it sounds, consider selling and moving to a less expensive home.
3. Are you currently making a car payment? If so, commit to keeping the vehicle long enough to pay it off and then at least three to four years longer so that you can save enough money to buy your next vehicle with cash.

WHAT THE WORD SAYS

Is there anyone here who, planning to build a new house, doesn't first sit down and figure the cost so you'll know if you can complete it? (Luke 14:28, MSG)

Chapter 11

TEACHING MONEY TO DANCE: PART 2

How can we know the dancer from the dance?

— WILLIAM BUTLER YEATS

Remember Susan from chapter 2? She tried to fill a void of loneliness by going on a shopping spree—buying a sports car and a fur and going on frequent vacations. Eventually she did get married, and she and her husband, Steve, embarked on a lifestyle that required two incomes: a large mortgage, car payments, and frequent restaurant meals. Then Steve lost his job, and the financial strain put pressure on their marriage. As they prayed for direction in their marriage and in Steve's career, they began to see that their spending was giving them short-term gratification while hurting something more important: their relationship. The birth of their daughter helped them further rethink their use of money. Today Susan has gone from a full-time sales career to part-time work for a nonprofit organization. She was able to make that change because of a series of financial decisions, both large and small.

When Steve's company transferred him across the country, he and Susan opted for a home with a mortgage payment two-thirds the size of their previous one. They cook many more meals than they used to, which saves on their food costs. They have found more inexpensive things to do for entertainment and vacations, such as visiting state parks and camping. They don't need to spend as much on child care or dry cleaning. Whereas Susan once had a personal shopper at Neiman Marcus, she now buys a lot of their clothes at Target. And they sold the Porsche long ago.

Susan acknowledges that some of their lifestyle changes have not come easily. However, as she puts it, "How can I put a value on the joy of walking my daughter to school every day?"

Exactly.

One reason so many people find it difficult to pursue goals that fulfill their true desires is lack of financial breathing space. What follows is a look at some of the most common expense categories, along with ideas on how to free up enough monthly margin to pursue more meaningful goals.

Uncle Sam

Some people go to extremes in their attempts to save on the amount of taxes they pay. There's the man who had been claiming his dog as a dependent for years; the man who had his furniture store torched after failing to sell it and then collected $500,000 from his insurance company, only to be caught when he tried to deduct the $10,000 he paid to the arsonist as a "consulting fee"; and the man who accidentally flushed his dentures down the toilet and then tried to claim the loss as an "act of God casualty loss."[1]

However, most people not only dutifully pay their fair share of income taxes, they *overpay*, giving Uncle Sam, in essence, a free loan. If you typically receive a tax refund, that's your situation. Around 80 percent of filers do just that, with the average refund totaling over $2,000.

The conventional wisdom about income taxes is that getting a refund is a good thing. People generally seem happy to get a big refund check. Some consider it to be a form of forced savings, and that's okay if you can't save otherwise and as long as the refund goes straight into a savings or investment account. In most cases, though, it's better to stop being so benevolent toward the government. While it's true that generosity is part of our design, I'm a bigger fan of giving to organizations that need the money rather than to one that can literally print its own.

If you usually get a tax refund, estimate how much you should be paying in taxes by using the IRS online calculator (go to www.irs.gov and search on "Withholding Calculator"). If you find that you're overpaying, talk to the human resources or payroll department where you work and have your withholding adjusted accordingly.

If you're self-employed, be sure to set aside money each month in order to pay your estimated quarterly taxes. Treat this as near-term *When* savings, just like an annual insurance bill or a semiannual real estate tax bill, where you put enough money in savings each month to cover the taxes when they are due.

Wires and Pipes

Take a good look at all the electric outlets, light switches, oven knobs, and water faucets in your home. To be sure, the wires and pipes behind them are the conduits through which some very vital stuff—electricity, gas, and water—flows into your home. But they are also the conduits through which a lot of money unnecessarily flows out of your home. Here are a few ideas for saving on the cost of utilities.

1. Unplug. You may be able to save up to 25 percent on your electric bill just by cutting down on "standby loss." Think of all the items you leave plugged in when you're not using them—televisions, computers, printers, coffeemakers—and get in the habit of pulling the plug when they're idle. Or plug multiple devices into a power strip and get in the habit of turning it off when the devices aren't in use.

2. Automate. Install a programmable thermostat that automatically lowers your home's temperature (in the winter) overnight while you're sleeping and then raises it just before you get up.

3. Buy better bulbs. As your lightbulbs burn out, replace them with compact fluorescent ones (CFL). A 25-watt CFL produces as much light as a 100-watt conventional bulb but uses one-quarter the energy. They cost a bit more than regular bulbs (although prices have come down), but they last a lot longer. One word of caution: CFLs contain mercury, so don't throw burned-out bulbs in the trash. Contact your local waste disposal company for information on how to dispose of CFLs properly.

4. Slow the flow. Replace standard 4.5-gallons-per-minute shower-heads with those that use 2.5 GPM. Making the switch can save up to 20,000 gallons of water per year.

Chow

The average household spends almost 45 percent of its food dollars on restaurant meals.[2] Eat at home more often and you will save money. Some of the best ways to save on your food bill include all of the usual suspects: making and sticking to a shopping list, buying private-label products, using coupons, bringing your lunch to work — effective ideas you've probably heard before. Here are a few others you may not have tried.

1. Take the aisle less traveled. Break out of your routine and do some grocery shopping in dollar stores, discount grocery stores, or the grocery aisles of mass merchandisers such as Target or Wal-Mart. Drugstores now offer a greater variety of food products and often offer great discounts on milk and other food items.

2. Cherry-pick. It's easy to get in a rut and buy groceries at just one or two stores. Besides, we figure it's a better use of our time to consolidate our shopping in as few stores as possible. However, a detailed study published by the Wharton School of the University of Pennsylvania found that cherry-picking (the practice of going from store to store, buying only each store's most deeply discounted items in a given week) is worth the investment of our time. Just be sure to buy items you really need, and if it's a nonperishable item, stock up.[3]

3. Make a price book. Use a small notepad to create a list of the items you buy most often and the best prices per ounce or per count you have found. Keep it with you as you shop so you will know when you're getting the best deal. A price book is especially helpful when you shop in an unfamiliar store to pick up an item that's on deep discount. As you consider other products while you're there, which the retailer hopes you will, a price book will help you see if the store's prices on other items are good deals or not.

4. Don't overdo the organics. Organic foods are growing in popularity, but they can cost much more than nonorganic alternatives. According to *Consumer Reports*, some organic products are worth their higher cost because the nonorganic versions contain harmful levels of chemicals. Others are not worth it because the nonorganic versions typically don't have detectable amounts of pesticides.

The following chart shows which foods *Consumer Reports* says are worth paying a premium for their organic versions and which ones are not worth the extra money.

Worth Going Organic	Not Worth Going Organic
Apples	Asparagus
Baby food	Avocados
Beef	Bananas
Bell peppers	Bread
Celery	Broccoli
Cherries	Canned fruit and vegetables
Dairy products	Cauliflower
Imported grapes	Cereal
Nectarines	Kiwi
Peaches	Mangos
Pears	Oils
Potatoes	Onions
Poultry	Papaya
Red raspberries	Pasta
Spinach	Pineapples
Strawberries	Potato chips
	Sweet corn
	Sweet peas

Consumer Reports also recommends taking a pass on organic seafood because the lack of organic certification standards for seafood means that seafood labeled as organic may not be any freer of contaminants than nonorganic seafood.

For most people, food is one of their most frequent expenditures and one of their largest spending categories overall. Fortunately, we have a lot of choices in where to shop for food and how.

Threads

When I was digging myself into debt, I shopped at some of the most interesting (and expensive) clothing stores in Chicago. Even after I hit bottom and started clawing my way back to financial solvency, I preferred to shop the sales of some of the "better" department stores. I rationalized that I was buying quality clothes on discount.

I've since discovered that you can get quality clothes at even better prices if you shop at stores like TJ Maxx, Marshalls, Ross Dress for Less, and Target. As I suggested with groceries, go into stores you may never have tried. You'll be surprised at the quality you can find for a fraction of what the "better" stores charge.

I've also learned to look for clothing that's likely to last a while, which means well-made clothing and less trendy, more classic clothing. I also try to buy clothing that does not need dry cleaning.

If you have young kids, who will outgrow clothes quickly, shop used-clothing stores, rummage sales, and garage sales, especially in more expensive neighborhoods. A friend of ours, Jennifer, found most of the clothing her young son will need for the next two years for a total of twelve dollars. How did she do it? First, she got "huge" amounts of clothing through the free section of craigslist.org. Next, she hit two "jackpot" rummage/yard sales in which she bought about three dozen items for her son at an average price of thirty-three cents each, including brand-name clothing in great condition. Jennifer also recommends going to the last day of a rummage sale, bringing a large bag, and offering five dollars for however much you can fit into the bag.

Another site where you can find everything from free clothing to free furniture is www.freecycle.org.

Baubles

As I said earlier, gift giving is one of the top budget killers. Many of us overspend on gifts, especially during the year-end holiday season. Retailers generate 20 percent of their annual volume from the year-end holidays,[4] and they pull out all the stops to generate that volume. Here are four ways you can resist their overtures for you to overspend.

1. Be like Santa. No one ever accused old St. Nick of not planning ahead. Every Christmas, he makes a list and even checks it twice. Taking a lesson from his playbook can help us survive the holidays and other gift-giving occasions in better financial shape. Make a list of the people you typically buy gifts for, estimating how much you plan to spend on each. Use the form on the next page. Take the total you plan to spend for the year, even if most of the spending will occur at the end of the year, divide by twelve, and then enter that amount on your budget. On months when you don't spend that much, money will build up in your checking account so that you'll have it when you need it.

2. Be like Scrooge. I'm not suggesting you take Scrooge-like behavior to the extremes of, well, Scrooge. However, think back to last year's Christmas or your last birthday. What presents did you get? If you can remember even one or two items, you're doing better than most people. Chances are you can't remember most of what you've received over the years. And here's the really bad news: neither can the recipients of the gifts you've given. So try to identify at least one person — more, if you can — who you could approach with this suggestion: "Let's stop exchanging gifts on our birthdays and at Christmas." This isn't about stinginess; it's about sanity. You'll both save time by not having to shop for each other, and you'll save money. My guess is there are people in your life who will welcome such a suggestion. Then again, there are some who won't. For those, read on.

Gift List

Person	Birthday	Christmas	Other	Other	Total
1.					
2.					
3.					
4.					
5.					
6.					
7.					
8.					
9.					
10.					
Grand Total					$

3. Be yourself. Are you a woodworker or a seamstress? I'm not proposing that you create a second career devoted to making people gifts, but if it's a hobby you engage in anyway, why not make gifts for your friends and family? Most people will value something you make for them more than something you buy for them, and you can likely make something that will be a lot less expensive than buying a sweater that may not be the right size or color.

4. Be an early bird. If you insist on store-bought gifts, instead of waking yourself from a turkey-induced coma the morning after Thanksgiving and then elbowing your way past the crowds clamoring for discounted DVD players, buy gifts throughout the year. You're much more likely to find good options on sale if you do your shopping well before the holidays.

Monday Brunch

On a recent vacation, Jude and I agreed to splurge on Sunday brunch at a famous hotel. Then we called to find out the price and decided that making our next mortgage payment was more important. But we also discovered that the hotel offered a similar brunch during the week at a fraction of the cost, so we went out for Monday brunch instead. So "Monday brunch" has become my term for buying entertainment on discount. Here are a few other ideas for how to do this.

1. Dining for fewer dollars. For many people, a nice restaurant meal is a favored form of entertainment. To minimize the cost, why not go out for lunch instead of dinner? Or, if you're going out for dinner, go early to a restaurant that offers discounted meals before a certain time. Order water to drink — tap water, that is — instead of a soft drink. If you are planning to have wine with your meal, consider a restaurant where you can bring your own bottle.

2. Experience culture for free. Heading out to a museum? Our family enjoys living close to Chicago, home to some world-class museums. As is true in most major cities, the museums here are free on certain days. If you have a large family or are going with a group of friends, seek out the free days and you will save a lot of money.

3. Borrow your books; don't own them. Do you like to read? We don't have enough space on our bookshelves for all of our books. Slowly, we're giving some away; we've even sold some on eBay. As we pare down our collection, I've come to realize that although there are some books I do prefer to own, I can get all that I want from most books by checking them out of our local library. We're paying for those books anyway with our taxes, so we might as well read them. Many libraries also offer good selections of movies on DVD that are available for checkout.

4. Stay on the cutting edge — of last year's trends. Do you play a sport? If so, you know the temptation to buy all the latest gear "guaranteed" to take your performance to the next level. If you're really into your sport, you should have such equipment — a year or two after it's introduced. That's when you'll find it on the clearance rack or in a store that sells used sports equipment. My golf bag contains nothing but high-quality, name-brand golf clubs — all purchased at a deep discount at used golf equipment shops or during year-end clearance sales at mainline stores.

5. Cut the cable. Over the years, I've met with many people in search of more breathing room in their monthly budgets who say they've already looked at their spending from every possible angle and can't find any more financial fat on the bone. However, in most cases, they're paying for cable or satellite television or TiVo. These have become necessary expenses in many people's minds. But are they? Cutting these will, of course, save you the cost of the monthly fees. It's also likely to cause you to watch less television, and that will save you even more money. A study done by Juliet Schor of Boston College found that the more television we watch, the less we save. Apparently, with more exposure to commercials and programs featuring people living expensive lifestyles, we tend to spend more.[5] If you can't bring yourself to cut the cable completely, at least consider switching to a less expensive package.

The Wallet/Body Connection

I'm sure it isn't news to you that health-related costs are getting out of control, whether it's the cost of health insurance, the size of your co-pay, or the amount of your deductibles. Here are two suggestions for keeping medical costs down.

1. Take care of yourself. If you don't get regular exercise, a little is a lot better than none. Start taking short walks after dinner, for example. You'll feel better, and you may even find yourself spending less on doctor's bills. Another benefit, as long as you walk with someone else, is improved relationships, and that's one of the primary sources of happiness.

2. Take advantage of a flexible spending account (FSA) or a health savings account (HSA). Such accounts enable you to set aside pretax money for medical expenses not covered by insurance, such as co-pays and deductibles. You can also use FSA money for day care and even summer day camp expenses for your kids. With HSAs, you must have a high-deductible health insurance plan, but HSA money can be rolled over from year to year. Join the small minority who utilize such accounts and you'll save money. Look at my website (www.moneypurposejoy.com) for links to sites with more information about both types of accounts.

More Wise Money Moves

Those are a few of my favorite tactics for spending more effectively on the stuff we all buy. What follows are some strategic approaches to spending smarter.

Keep Up with the Smiths

Who are the Smiths, you wonder? They're the folks who live on the other side of town from the Joneses. Whereas the Jones family may have the outwardly enviable lifestyle—the latest clothes, cars, and such—the Smiths have the more completely enviable lifestyle. They're not living in shacks or driving beaters, but they buy what they can afford and live with enough margin to be able to give generously and save for their most important goals. It pays to seek out such role models.

Shortly after we moved into our current home, we got some estimates for turning our backyard deck into a combination sunroom/office. It would have been a much more comfortable and inspiring place for me to write than our basement. While the thought of working with a view of our peaceful backyard excited me, Jude and I both had some reservations. We had a healthy cushion of savings, but we didn't know how quickly my writing and speaking work would grow. The extra living space would be nice, but maybe we would be better off keeping the money in savings. We went back and forth several times.

In the midst of that decision-making process, we had a couple over for dinner who we had wanted to get to know better. Money-related conversations have a habit of breaking out around me, and that night was no exception. Rob is a pilot for a major airline, yet he and Amy live in a small two-bedroom townhouse. That night, they said they had no immediate plans to move, even though they were then expecting their second child. Somewhere in the conversation, we also confirmed a rumor that their television has a thirteen-inch screen (although reports about it being black-

and-white turned out to be greatly exaggerated!).

Rob and Amy explained that living below their means gives them great freedom and flexibility. When the airline Rob works for got into financial trouble several years ago and made significant cuts to all of the pilots' salaries, they weathered the storm without any significant changes to their lifestyle. By contrast, many of Rob's colleagues had to sell homes they could no longer afford. After hearing their story, Jude and I decided to keep the deck-conversion money in savings.

We need more role models like Rob and Amy. The problem is that most of us don't typically talk about our financial dealings, even with our closest friends. But we can change. Which of your friends seem to manage their money especially well? I'm not talking about the ones with the flashiest cars and the latest cell phones; I'm talking about the ones who seem to be living beneath their means. Ask them about some of their financial choices. If you ease into the conversation, chances are they'll be happy to explain why they've made certain decisions. And some of their thinking just may rub off on you.

Hurry Up and Wait

Everything in our culture, it seems, tells us to hurry up, especially as it relates to spending money. Dieticians, however, offer a counterprinciple that has application for wise money management. Whether we're trying to lose weight or not, we would all be wise to let our food settle for a little while before going for that second helping. Apparently, the brain is slow to understand just how full we really are. Press the pause button before heading back to the buffet and we will probably take a pass on that second piece of pie.

The same is true with many purchase decisions. Wait a little while, and the urge to spend may pass. In many cases, choosing to sleep on a spending decision or to just walk away for a little while helps us realize we'd be better off *without* that extra sweater.

Think Dollars, Not Percentages

When it comes to giving and saving, it's best to think in terms of percentages, basing each on a percentage of income. Not so with buying things on sale, at least not exclusively. In this case, think in terms of absolute dollars. Here's why: Researchers have found that most of us are willing to drive across town to save $50 on what would normally be $100 worth of groceries (Wow, 50 percent off!) but not on the purchase of a $20,000 automobile (A lousy fifty bucks? Who cares?). This makes no sense, because, after all, fifty dollars saved is fifty dollars saved.

Mouse Around

The Internet offers all sorts of possibilities for saving both money and time, especially through the use of comparison-shopping sites. Enter the name and model number of a product you're considering buying and up will pop a list of sellers and their prices. You'll be surprised at how the price for the same item varies. Check out the "Links" page within the "Resources" tab of my website (www.moneypurposejoy.com) for the most current list of recommended sites.

When making an online purchase, you will often see a box where you can enter a promotion code. But where do you get the code? An entire cottage industry of coupon code websites has emerged to answer that question. Do a Google search for "coupon codes" and you'll see what I mean. Here again, check my website for my most recent recommended sites.

Improve Your Number

Do you know your credit score? That three-digit number impacts your ability to get a job, qualify for the best rate on a mortgage and the best price on insurance, and more. Just as doctors encourage us to keep tabs on our cholesterol, we should keep tabs on our credit score and proactively work to keep it healthy. Here's what to do.

1. Order your free credit report. Note that I said *report*, not *score*. Your report, which is used to determine your score, is free. Your score, maddeningly, is not. To get a free report from each of the three main credit bureaus, go to www.annualcreditreport.com and follow the instructions. If you prefer dialing to surfing, call 877-322-8228.

2. Read your report. It is estimated that nearly 80 percent of credit reports contain an error, such as an outdated address or closed accounts marked as open. If you notice an error, file a dispute with the credit bureau (instructions for doing so are provided on the report) and then notify the creditor. If you suspect fraud — maybe you see a credit card you never opened — contact the creditor immediately. Then call one of the credit bureaus to place a ninety-day fraud alert on your report. A call to one bureau will trigger the alert at the others. You might also consider freezing your credit. The rules and regulations related to credit freezes are changing rapidly. For the latest info, go to the Federal Trade Commission's website at www.ftc.gov and search on "Credit Freeze."

3. Buy your score. Yes, it seems unfair that you have to pay, but that's just how it is. Some of the credit bureaus have their own method of calculating your score. What you really need is your FICO (stands for "Fair Isaac Corporation," inventor of the credit risk score used by most lenders) score. It should cost less than $20.

4. Manage your number. Scores range from 300 to 850. Unlike cholesterol, the higher the number the better. The best way to keep your credit score high is to pay your bills on time. Many banks offer free online bill payment, and that can be helpful in paying bills on time. See if your bank offers free online bill payment.

Put Your Blessings in a Box

Do you remember Bob and Jody from chapter 7? They had been saving to replace an old van, but their desire to adopt a child prompted them to use that money for the adoption fees. When a relative unexpectedly gave them a van, Bob and Jody wrote a note about the experience and put it in what they call a blessing box. They do this throughout the year whenever some unexpected blessing occurs. Then at Thanksgiving, they read the notes and remember God's goodness — all of the blessings, large and small, that happened throughout the year. It's a meaningful time for Bob and Jody, and they hope the tradition fosters hearts of gratitude and contentment in the lives of their children.

In a culture that does its best to foster discontentment — the more the better to keep us on the treadmill of "want, spend, and want some more" — maybe the blessing box is the best money management idea of all.

Putting the Ideas into Action

We've covered a lot of ideas for spending more effectively, for teaching money to dance to the tune of our true desires — so many, in fact, that you may be a bit overwhelmed. Keep in mind that you don't need to implement all of these ideas, and you certainly don't need to implement them all at once. Ease into them, incorporating more over time. Refer to these chapters from time to time to remind yourself of ideas you may have forgotten. And one more money-saving idea is to sign up for my free e-newsletters that are available from my website. I'm constantly looking for ideas on how to manage money more effectively, and twice a month I share the best ideas I've found via my e-newsletters.

WHAT TO REMEMBER

1. Spending effectively is not about being a tightwad; it's about making choices that enable us to live with financial margin.
2. Big savings can be gained from some simple changes, such as exploring different stores than you may be accustomed to for groceries and clothing, raising the deductibles on your automobile insurance (as long as you have money saved in your *If* fund), and planning ahead for gift buying.
3. There are other helpful habits as well, such as finding positive money-management role models, walking away from a potential purchase long enough to see if the purchase is really in your best interest, and using the Internet to compare prices.

WHAT TO DO

1. This chapter listed a variety of ways to save money on many common spending categories. Pick at least one idea and try it this week.

2. Make a list of people you plan to buy gifts for this year and then use the same list to create a gift budget. Make sure you're saving one-twelfth of the annual amount each month. Also, consider whether you could approach any people on the list with the idea of not exchanging gifts.

3. Order your credit report and check it for mistakes. If you find any, report them right away. Purchase your score as well. Remember that the best step you can take to keeping your score high is to pay all of your bills on time.

WHAT THE WORD SAYS

Life is not measured by how much you own. (Luke 12:15, NLT)

Chapter 12

TRAVELING IN FINANCIAL COMMUNITY

The life I touch for good or ill will touch another life, and
that in turn another, until who knows where the trembling
stops or in what far place my touch will be felt.

— FREDERICK BUECHNER

As with most golfers, I prefer to play when the winds are calm, the skies clear, and the temperature comfortable. Except for a few clouds, that's how it was at the beginning of one memorable round of golf with a good friend. Not long after we started, however, more clouds began to form. Suddenly the sky became dark and ominous. As rain began to fall, Jeff and I headed for shelter underneath some nearby trees. Before we knew it, lightning started flashing and we realized we were not in a safe place. Since we were too far away to make a run for the clubhouse, we looked around for another option and spotted a slightly oversized outhouse that looked to be made of plastic. Quickly the rain turned into a downpour, the lightning became more intense, and the winds grew stronger. Leaving our golf bags where they were, we made a run for it. When we got there, two people were already taking shelter inside.

So there we stood, four people huddled in an outhouse, keeping the door open as much as possible, despite the heavy rain, in an unsuccessful attempt to minimize the stench. We were stuck there for more than two hours as the thunder boomed and lightning rained down from the sky.

While it was not the most comfortable place to hang out for an afternoon, what could have been a frightening experience was made much less so by the company of others. There's encouragement in community, in sharing the journey, no matter how scary—or how smelly!

We may not have been meant to do life together in outhouses, but we were definitely meant to do life together. When we travel in financial community, we are expressing the other-centeredness that lies at the heart of what it means to be a *Builder*: making a difference in people's lives.

There are five elements of traveling in financial community:

1. Living in financial truth
2. Influencing others
3. Sharing with others
4. Teaching others
5. Spurring each other on

Some elements may feel uncomfortable, at least at first, but each is designed to help us experience uncommon financial success and joy. The essential first step is to take an honest look at our own financial situation.

Living in Financial Truth

As he reflected on the story of civil rights leader Rosa Parks, Parker Palmer said that Parks' decision to sit in the "whites-only" section of a public bus was based on her conviction to live out of who she was. She was tired of acting on the outside in a way that contradicted the truth she held deeply on the inside.[1]

As we discussed in chapter 2, it's all too easy to find ourselves behaving in a way that contradicts our true financial situation or our true desires. When we spend more money than we make, we contradict the truth of our financial situation. When we say we believe in certain causes, yet our spending prohibits us from supporting those causes, we contradict our true desires. Managing money this way wears on our wallets and hinders our happiness.

The Bible tells us that the truth will set us free,[2] and living in financial truth will do the same. Living in financial truth means buying homes, cars, clothing, and such based on a plan that enables us to live within our means. It means managing money in a way that enables us to strengthen our most valued relationships, make a meaningful contribution with our lives, and honor God.

When we live in financial truth, money becomes a source of joy rather than stress and no longer gets in the way of our hearing God's call on our lives. It also enables us to have a positive influence on others.

Influencing Others

The Bible teaches us to always be ready to give an explanation for our faith, saying, "Be prepared to give an answer to everyone who asks you to give the reason for the hope that you have."[3] The assumption is that our faith will be so evident that people will ask questions. In *The Journey of Desire*, John Eldredge wonders,

> When was the last time someone stopped you to inquire about the reason for the hope that lies within you? You're at the market, say, in the frozen food section. A friend you haven't seen for some time comes up to you, grasps you by both shoulders, and pleads, "Please, you've got to tell me. Be honest now. How can you live with such hope? Where does it come from? I must know the reason."[4]

I laughed when I first read that. And then I cringed. Has there *ever* been such a time? In a similar vein, when was the last time any of our financial decisions attracted someone's curiosity because they express a different set of priorities than most people have? In the previous chapter, I suggested seeking out positive financial role models. Now I'm suggesting that we *become* positive financial role models.

When our financial decisions reflect our true desires to enhance our relationships, make a meaningful contribution, and honor God, others are likely to notice there's something different about our lives. Just keeping a car for more than five years qualifies as unusual behavior; keeping one for ten years or more will attract attention. So is using some of your vacation time and your hard-earned money to serve with a ministry you support. Although your motivation for doing so is not about calling attention to yourself, such a decision is likely to prompt questions that can lead to potentially life-changing conversations.

Think about what could happen if you began making financial choices designed to help resolve some festering conflict in your marriage and if you were willing to share your journey with others. Let's say you realize that your habit of carrying a balance on your credit cards is getting in the way of saving and that living with no margin is leading to frequent arguments. What if you decided to make some changes in how much you spend on entertainment so that you could start saving and stop fighting? It would certainly improve the quality of your marriage. But what if you took it a step further? Imagine that friends invite you to join them for dinner at an expensive restaurant and you suggest making a meal together at your home instead. Not only will it be a better financial move but it may also offer an opportunity to tell them about your motivation. It isn't about being cheap, you explain; it's about enjoying time with friends while also being able to enjoy more margin and less stress. That may get them thinking about doing the same thing.

What about a seemingly simple decision to drive your car a bit longer? If that helps you save enough money to make the career move that's been tugging at your heart for so long, couldn't that motivate others who feel called to do the same thing?

While I'm not encouraging you to broadcast these decisions to everyone you meet, people notice what we do with our money, and they're influenced by those decisions (how else would we have heard about Rob and Amy's thirteen-inch television, which I mentioned in the previous chapter?).

When *Consumers* make more money, it seems only natural for them to buy bigger homes and nicer cars. In fact, it seems as though there's no other option. However, because as *Builders* our identities and happiness are not dependent on what we own, we're free to choose a different path. Exercising that freedom may turn out to be the best move for our finances, and for the finances of our friends.

While we're certainly not responsible for the decisions other people make, our decisions do have an impact on them. Allow that recognition to play a role in your decision making.

One way we can have a positive influence on others is the third element of traveling in financial community: sharing our resources.

Sharing with Others

Have you ever walked through your neighborhood on a spring day and looked inside other people's garages? Don't the contents look familiar? Don't they look remarkably similar to the contents of your own garage? I'm not suggesting that you form a commune, but couldn't we do a better job of sharing?

On a recent teaching trip to the East Coast, I had dinner at the home of some new friends. In their yard stood a pile of mulch. A *big* pile of mulch. It turns out that Jason and Pam had gone in on the purchase with their neighbor. In part, it was a money-saving idea, since they split the cost of delivery. But it was also an opportunity to build a relationship with their neighbor — "an opportunity for us to meet at the fence" is how they put it.

What if we all started looking for more opportunities to "meet at the fence"? Instead of every family buying its own swing set or inflatable pool, what if several families went in on such purchases together? Instead of all the gardeners renting their own rototillers to work on their vegetable patches, what if we rented one together for a day and shared it? We'd probably save money, and we just might make some friends along the way.

Think of your own family for a minute. Do all the drivers in your household really need their own cars? As I mentioned earlier, there are now more vehicles per household than licensed drivers. Sure, it's more convenient for everyone to have his or her own set of wheels. But wouldn't it strengthen your finances if you didn't have so many cars to pay for, maintain, and insure? Couldn't it strengthen your relationships if you had to share, working together to manage who needs the car when?

In addition to sharing our resources, traveling in financial community involves sharing with others—particularly with young people—some of the lessons we're learning about wise money management.

Teaching Others

For many years, the Jump$tart Coalition has been surveying twelfth graders, measuring their financial literacy. In 1997, the average student answered 57 percent of the questions correctly—a failing score. Since then, things have gotten worse. In 2008, the average high school senior answered 48 percent of the questions correctly.[5] If you have kids at home, the most effective way to teach them how to manage money well is to model wise money management. The second is by talking with them about money—explaining why you use a budget, showing them how it works, and walking them through the benefits of buying used sports equipment instead of new, for example, so that money can be saved for the next family vacation.

Tell others about these principles as well—relatives, friends, neighbors, and coworkers. Doing so will reinforce the lessons in your own life, and as you see the positive impact on others, it will be a source of joy.

Finally, traveling in financial community involves support and accountability from a small group of like-minded friends.

Spurring Each Other On

Our culture offers little encouragement for the principles we've been discussing throughout this book. We're not likely to drive by billboards telling us to hang on to our current car for ten years and buy our next one with cash. Nor are we likely to hear a radio commercial promoting the simple pleasures of taking a bike ride with a good friend—that is, not unless the ride takes place in an expensive vacation area sponsoring the commercial. That's why we need accountability and encouragement partners.

If you want to manage money well, find a small group of people with whom you can go where few people dare to go: into a conversation about money. Get together regularly (at least every other week) to discuss the ideas in this book (consider using the companion discussion guide to help facilitate your discussions). Talk about money within the context of your true desires. Discuss the decisions you're contemplating and give and receive counsel, accountability, and encouragement. Share your goals and concerns, talk about your victories and setbacks, and spur each other on.[6] Not only will your finances improve, your friendships will deepen as well.

Make a list today of the people you'd consider inviting to join your group. If you can come up with only one person, that's okay. Start there. Eventually, others will likely come to mind. If it feels awkward, at least at first, that's how it should feel. Keep in mind that you don't have to bare your entire financial soul in the first meeting. Ease into it. Get to know each other first. What sort of financial lessons, both good and bad, did you learn from your parents? What financial goals do you have? What challenges do you face? Over time, as trust is built, share more details of your financial lives. Social psychologist David Myers says, "Disclosure begets disclosure. I reveal more to you if you have first been open with me."[7] As you start to talk about your financial life, your accountability and encouragement partners will feel freer to share with you.

Opening the Door to a New World

At the end of the movie *The Truman Show*, Truman Burbank discovers that he has been living on a giant stage in front of millions of television viewers around the world. All of the people he encountered in his life—including his own wife, his best friend, his neighbors, and his work associates—turned out to be paid actors. He was the only one who wasn't in on the joke.

In the final scene, he is sailing a small boat, desperately trying to escape that false world. Because even the water on which he is sailing is part of the stage, control room technicians are able to manufacture a fierce storm to stop him. Finally, the sea is made calm and Truman drifts into a wall that had been painted to look like the horizon. There he discovers a stairway leading to a door. As he climbs the stairs, a godlike voice from above calls his name.

"Who are you?" Truman asks.

"I am the creator of a television show that gives hope and joy and inspiration to millions."

"And who am I?"

"You are the star."

"Was nothing real?"

"You were real. It's what made you so good to watch. Listen to me, Truman. There's no more truth out there than there is in the world I created for you. Same lies, same deceit. But in my world, you have nothing to fear. I know you better than you know yourself."

"You've never had a camera in my head."

"You're afraid. That's why you can't leave. It's okay, Truman. I understand. I've been watching you your whole life. I was watching when you were born. I was watching when you took your first step. I've watched you on your first day in school. You can't leave, Truman. You belong here with me."[8]

With that, Truman opens the door and walks off the stage, eagerly turning his back on the false world in which he had been living.

When we choose to travel the financial path toward home, we open the door to a whole new world. We stop settling for the false world of props and pretenses, of financial fronts and consumerist comparisons, and we begin living in financial truth. We stop living in relationship *to* other people and start living in relationship *with* other people. We're no longer quick to accept the conventional wisdom about how much to spend on homes and cars and a night out. Now we make those decisions within the context of our true desires to build into our most valued relationships, make a meaningful contribution with our lives, and honor God. We have less debt and more savings, less stress and more joy. And we have a far greater appreciation for all that there is now to enjoy because we know that money and what it can buy are not the basis of our identity, value, happiness, or security. They are good gifts from God, who loves us more than we can even understand.

WHAT TO REMEMBER

1. There are five elements to traveling in financial community: living in financial truth, influencing others, sharing resources with others, teaching others, and spurring each other on in the wise use of money.
2. Traveling in financial community is about building relationships as much as it is about managing money well.
3. Many of the ideas in this book are countercultural. By traveling in financial community, especially by participating in a financial accountability and encouragement group, we can find the mutual support we need to put these ideas into practice.

WHAT TO DO

1. Assess the degree to which you are living in financial truth. Are you living within your means? Are you using money in a way that honors God, enhances your relationships, and enables you to make the difference that you feel called to make with your life?
2. Think of something you could share with someone else. It might be a ride to work, if only one day a week. How could this save you money? How could it help you build relationships?
3. Consider forming a financial accountability and encouragement group. Write down two or three potential members and then invite them to join you on the path toward uncommon financial success.

WHAT THE WORD SAYS

Don't look out only for your own interests, but take an interest in others, too. (Philippians 2:4, NLT)

WELCOME HOME

*Just think how happy you would be if you lost everything
you have now, and then got it back again.*

— FRANCES RODMAN

When the prodigal son returned home, it's a safe bet he was feeling more than his fair share of humility. After demanding an inheritance from his father in a brazen show of disrespect, he had squandered it all on wild living. That's what makes his father's response so moving.

> While he was still a long way off, his father saw him and was filled with compassion for him; he ran to his son, threw his arms around him and kissed him.
>
> The son said to him, "Father, I have sinned against heaven and against you. I am no longer worthy to be called your son."
>
> But the father said to his servants, "Quick! Bring the best robe and put it on him. Put a ring on his finger and sandals on his feet. Bring the fattened calf and kill it. Let's have a feast and celebrate. For this son of mine was dead and is alive again; he was lost and is found." So they began to celebrate.[1]

Since the father spotted his son while he was still a long way off, he must have been waiting, watching, hoping that his son would one day come home. When that day finally came, the father's joy could not be contained.

There were no "I told you so" lectures; there was no condemnation. There was an elderly dad *running* to greet his son. When at last they stood face-to-face, the father embraced his son and kissed him. Then he threw a party to celebrate the prodigal's return.

Our heavenly Father just as eagerly welcomes all of his prodigal sons and daughters when we return home. To be home is to live as we were designed to live: in relationship with God. Financially, it means making choices that enable us to build into the lives of the people we love, make a meaningful contribution with our lives, and honor God.

Maybe your turn toward home involves removing some of the financial stress from your relationships. Maybe it means getting out of debt, starting with a decision to incur no more consumer debt from this day forward. To be sure, this will take discipline and courage, it will take the loving but firm support of accountability and encouragement partners, and it will take trust that what may seem like an impossible task can, indeed, be accomplished. But just by thinking about becoming debt-free, can't you feel the weight starting to lift?

Maybe your turn toward home means pursuing the work you've been called to do, whether that means a different vocation, staying home with your kids, involvement in some kind of ministry, or something else. Perhaps the most productive step you could take toward that goal is to begin saving money so you can make such a move. It may rattle you to think about leaving the work you know how to do so well and for which you are so well paid, but if you are ever going to do what you were meant to do, you'll have to let go of what feels so secure. It might require driving your current car a little longer even though you've had your heart set on a new one. But isn't the chance to pursue the work you were meant to do way more important than a new car?

Maybe for you heading toward home means releasing the firm grip you've had on money—giving more to your church or another God-honoring organization that's tackling some of the world's most urgent needs. It may seem irrational to start investing in something that can't be measured with a price-to-earnings ratio. You may even wonder how much good your money can really do. But you know deep down that you were made to be generous; it's part of your design. And you sense that by loosening your grip on money, it will begin to release the hold it's had on you.

Have you wandered from home? Many of us have drifted in our use of money, making financial choices that get in the way of all that truly matters.

To return home, the prodigal son had to have a change of heart ("Father, I have sinned against heaven and against you. I am no longer worthy to be called your son"), make a conscious choice to move in a different direction ("I will set out and go back to my father"), and take action ("He got up and went to his father"). Those who long to live in financial freedom must do the same.

We must have a change of heart, flat out rejecting the identity of *Consumers* and embracing our true identity as *Builders*.

We must decide that following the conventional wisdom about money is not the proper path, for it leads us *away* from all that makes life meaningful; it leads us away from home. Instead, we must choose to set out down the path of using money in a way that strengthens our relationships, enables us to make a difference with our lives, and honors God. That involves giving generously, saving consistently, and spending in a way that gives us the financial breathing space to do all that.

We must take action, laying down the *Consumer's* primary tool of consumer debt while taking up the *Builder's* tool of a budget.

And we must do all of this in community, for only there will we be able to give and receive the encouragement we need in order to experience the success and joy we desire.

I don't know the specific plan God has for you — how he wants to use you in your family, your other relationships, and your work — but I know he *has* a plan for your life, a mission for you to fulfill. The financial ideas we've discussed will enable you to better discern it and get about the business of living it out.

I also know that when your primary commitment is to honor God and you make financial choices that reflect that commitment, there will be no "I told you so" lectures, no condemnation over past financial choices. Instead, there will be a joyful "welcome home" celebration, for the Owner of the house has been waiting for you, looking for you, hoping with all his heart that you would one day come home.

ACKNOWLEDGMENTS

It has been on my heart to write this book for more than ten years. Along the way, many people have provided wise counsel and other forms of invaluable assistance. If I have failed to acknowledge someone in what follows, it is not due to a lack of gratitude, only the lack of a better memory.

To Brian Nakaerts, Dave Bunge, and Skip Galanes, thank you for your helpful guidance on insurance, tax, and cost-of-living questions, respectively.

To Nancy Heche, thank you for a powerful and helpful afternoon sharing your book-writing journey with me.

To Paul Harris, thank you for helping me navigate the twin valleys of grief and fear at a critical time in the writing of this book.

To the many friends and family members who provided words of encouragement or prayed for me as I wrote, thank you. They include my brother, Dave; my in-laws, Ken and Barb, Jim and Kirsten, and Doug; Bret and Becky Petkus; Craig and Laurie Steensma; Dave and Emily Reuter; Dale and Steve Tombs; Jim and Jill Sharkey; Rob and Amy Cataldo; Paul and Sheila Jenkinson; Keith and Caroline Wilson; Randy and Diane Virden; Sibyl Towner; Bill Hayes; Sue Krause; Paula Haun; and the Riverside women's prayer group.

To Jim Sharkey, thank you for seeing the words "Money. Purpose. Joy." on my business card and exclaiming, "That's it—that should be the title of your book!"

To all who read various drafts of the manuscript—including

Todd Anderson, Scott Clifton, Jackson Crum, Laurie Steensma, and Tom Vislisel—thank you for taking the time and for your invaluable feedback.

To Dave Briggs, thank you for taking the time to read several versions of the manuscript and then talking me through your feedback. I greatly respect your knowledge, passion for this topic, and opinions. You have had a strong and helpful influence on my thinking and writing.

To Rob Gaskill, thank you for taking the initiative to introduce Jude and me to Dwight and Betty Nelson. Dwight, thank you for your many helpful comments on the manuscript, and thanks to you and Betty for introducing us to Randy and Debbie Birkey. Randy and Debbie, thank you for opening a vitally important door for me.

To Robert, Andrew, and Erik Wolgemuth, thank you for taking a chance on a new author, especially at a time when your literary agency was "not officially taking new clients." It's an honor to be represented by you. Erik, thanks for your determination—for hearing "maybe" when the actual word spoken was "no." Thanks as well for your wise guidance, words of encouragement, and prayers.

To Dan Benson at NavPress, thank you for your willingness to take a risk and the always-upbeat tone of your notes. Working with you has been a privilege and a pleasure.

To Liz Heaney, thank you for your masterful editing of this book. The title "editor" doesn't begin to do justice to who you are and what you do. Your ideas have challenged my thinking and shaped this into a far better book than it ever could have been without your help.

To everyone who trusted me with some of the details of your money story, thank you. I pray that your stories will encourage all who read them as much as they have encouraged me.

To Wayne Riendeau, thank you for getting back in touch and challenging me to think about matters of faith. In doing so, you helped change the direction of my life.

To Joe Ruh, John Fuhler, Justin Traver, and Mark Salavitch, thanks for all of the laughter over the years, and even the tears. Your characteristically gentle suggestion—"Either start writing the book you've been talking about for the last ten years or stop talking about it!" — got me going.

To Warren Beach, thank you for introducing me to what the Bible says about money. You helped spark a passion that has become my life's work.

To Dick Towner, thank you for your friendship and all the mentoring you've poured into me. By instruction and example, you have shaped my life in countless good ways. When I think of what it means to be a man after God's own heart, I think of you. I plan to keep hanging around in the hope that more of you will rub off on me.

To my parents, Jerry and Louise Bell. They instilled in me a love of learning and teaching, and they encouraged me to follow my dreams. How I wish they had lived to see my dream of writing this book fulfilled. I know they would have been very proud, as it will always be that I am their son.

To my sons, Jonathan and Andrew. To a casual observer, it probably looks as if parents do everything for their young children. But that couldn't be further from the truth. Just by being my sons you do far more for me, filling me with more happiness than I thought possible. Thanks for all of the "interruptions" while I wrote so that we could play "faster, faster," jump on the bed, or look for pictures of fire trucks on the Internet.

Mostly, to my wife, Jude. When we first met, I was amazed at the strength of your faith and the tenderness of your heart. After nine years of marriage, I am only more amazed, and ever more thankful to be your husband. How many wives would think it's a good idea for their husband to leave a well-paying corporate job (with benefits!) to take their family down a much more uncertain path? You were not only willing to go on the adventure, you were eager. During my moments of greatest doubt and deepest discouragement, you knew just what to say to lift my spirits. And with each bit of good news, your delight multiplied mine. This book would not have been possible without you. Every good thing that has ever happened in my life pales in comparison to the joy of being married to you.

RECOMMENDED MONTHLY SPENDING GUIDELINES

(Three-Person Household)

Annual Gross Income	$30,000		$45,000		$60,000	
Monthly Gross Income	$2,500		$3,750		$5,000	
Giving	$250	10.0%	$375	10.0%	$500	10.0%
Saving/Investing	$250	10.0%	$375	10.0%	$500	10.0%
Consumer Debts	$0	0%	$0	0%	$0	0%
Mortgage/Rent, Taxes, Insurance	$625	25.0%	$938	25.0%	$1,250	25.0%
Maintenance/Utilities	$150	6.0%	$244	6.5%	$325	6.5%
Transportation	$213	8.5%	$375	10.0%	$425	8.5%
Income Taxes	$240	9.6%	$424	11.3%	$665	13.3%
Food	$350	14.0%	$413	11%	$450	9.0%
Clothing	$47	1.9%	$83	2.2%	$150	3.0%
Other Household/ Personal	$50	2.0%	$75	2.0%	$100	2.0%
Entertainment	$38	1.5%	$75	2.0%	$125	2.5%
Health	$250	10.0%	$300	8.0%	$360	7.2%
Professional Services	$25	1.0%	$55	1.5%	$100	2.0%
Miscellaneous	$12	0.5%	$18	0.5%	$50	1.0%
Discretionary	$0	0%	$0	0%	$0	0%
Total	$2,500	100%	$3,750	100%	$5,000	100%

(Three-Person Household)

Annual Gross Income	$75,000		$90,000		$105,000	
Monthly Gross Income	$6,250		$7,500		$8,750	
Giving	$625	10.0%	$750	10.0%	$875	10.0%
Saving/Investing	$688	11.0%	$938	12.5%	$1,313	15.0%
Consumer Debts	$0	0%	$0	0%	$0	0%
Mortgage/Rent, Taxes, Insurance	$1,563	25.0%	$1,868	24.9%	$2,170	24.8%
Maintenance/Utilities	$387	6.2%	$413	5.5%	$455	5.2%
Transportation	$438	7.0%	$450	6.0%	$455	5.2%
Income Taxes	$913	14.6%	$1,155	15.4%	$1,356	15.5%
Food	$500	8.0%	$563	7.5%	$586	6.7%
Clothing	$206	3.3%	$247	3.3%	$297	3.4%
Other Household/ Personal	$125	2.0%	$150	2.0%	$175	2.0%
Entertainment	$187	3.0%	$277	3.7%	$324	3.7%
Health	$406	6.5%	$397	5.3%	$420	4.8%
Professional Services	$150	2.4%	$225	3.0%	$254	2.9%
Miscellaneous	$62	1.0%	$67	0.9%	$70	0.8%
Discretionary	$0	0%	$0	0%	$0	0%
Total	$6,250	100%	$7,500	100%	$8,750	100%

(Three-Person Household)

	$120,000		$135,000		$150,000	
Annual Gross Income	$120,000		$135,000		$150,000	
Monthly Gross Income	$10,000		$11,250		$12,500	
Giving	$1,000	10.0%	$1,125	10.0%	$1,250	10.0%
Saving/Investing	$1,500	15.0%	$1,687	15.0%	$1,875	15.0%
Consumer Debts	$0	0%	$0	0%	$0	0%
Mortgage/Rent, Taxes, Insurance	$2,470	24.7%	$2,768	24.6%	$3,063	24.5%
Maintenance/Utilities	$475	4.75%	$495	4.4%	$525	4.2%
Transportation	$450	4.5%	$450	4.0%	$450	3.6%
Income Taxes	$1,540	15.4%	$1,834	16.3%	$2,075	16.6%
Food	$600	6.0%	$619	5.5%	$625	5.0%
Clothing	$380	3.8%	$405	3.6%	$437	3.5%
Other Household/ Personal	$260	2.6%	$292	2.6%	$350	2.8%
Entertainment	$400	4.0%	$450	4.0%	$500	4.0%
Health	$450	4.5%	$472	4.2%	$500	4.0%
Professional Services	$300	3.0%	$349	3.1%	$400	3.2%
Miscellaneous	$75	0.75%	$79	0.7%	$75	0.6%
Discretionary	$100	1.0%	$225	2.0%	$375	3.0%
Total	$10,000	100%	$11,250	100%	$12,500	100%

NOTES

Chapter 1: Wandering from Home

1. Luke 15:11-13.
2. Luke 15:14-16.
3. Luke 15:17-20.
4. Luke 15:20-24.
5. See Proverbs 3:5.
6. See Jeremiah 29:11.

Chapter 2: Financially True or False?

1. U.S. Department of Commerce Bureau of Economic Analysis, "National Economic Accounts," www.bea.gov/newsreleases/national/pi/pinewsrelease.htm.
2. Federal Reserve Board's Survey of Consumer Finances for 2004, "Recent Changes in U.S. Family Finances," http://www.federal-reserve.gov/pubs/bulletin/2006/financesurvey.pdf.
3. Pew Research Center, "We Try Hard. We Fall Short. Americans Assess Their Saving Habits," http://pewresearch.org/pubs/325/we-try-hard-we-fall-short-americans-assess-their-saving-habits.
4. National Opinion Research Center's General Social Survey, http://sda.berkeley.edu/archive.htm. Arthur C. Brooks, "The Left's 'Inequality' Obsession," *Wall Street Journal*, July 19, 2007, A15.
5. Erving Goffman, *The Presentation of Self in Everyday Life* (New York: Anchor Books, 1959), 27.
6. Thomas Stanley and William Danko, *The Millionaire Next Door* (Atlanta: Longstreet Press, 1996), 75.

7. Parker Palmer, *Let Your Life Speak* (San Francisco: Jossey-Bass, 2000), 32.

8. Palmer, 32–33.

Chapter 3: Why We've Settled for So Little

1. *Merriam-Webster's Collegiate Dictionary*, 10th ed., s.v. "consume."

2. *Oxford English Dictionary*, s.v. "*consumere*."

3. Juliet Schor, *The Overspent American* (New York: Basic Books, 1998), 57.

4. Schor, 70.

5. Schor, 229.

6. Pew Research Center, "Most Americans Moderately Upbeat About Family Finances in 2007," http://pewresearch.org/pubs/324/most-americans-moderately-upbeat-about-family-finances-in-2007.

7. 1 Timothy 6:10.

8. Genesis 1:27; 2:15 (NLT).

9. William Leach, *Land of Desire* (New York: Pantheon, 1993), 3.

10. Leach, 123.

11. Susan Strasser, *Satisfaction Guaranteed* (Washington, DC: Smithsonian Institution Press, 1989), 27.

12. Strasser, 89.

13. Leach, 66.

14. Juliet Schor, *The Overworked American* (New York: Basic Books, 1991), 119.

15. Leach, 124.

16. Strasser, 15.

17. Schor, *Overworked American*, 120.

18. Leach, 3.

19. Leach, 149.

20. Abbey Klaassen, "An Ad-Space Odyssey," *Advertising Age*, October 9, 2006.

21. David Myers, *The Pursuit of Happiness* (New York: Morrow, 1992), 51.

22. Schor, *Overworked American*, 123.

23. See Exodus 20:17.

24. Daniel Gilbert, *Stumbling on Happiness* (New York: Knopf, 2006), 217.

Chapter 4: What Truly Matters

1. Georg Simmel, *The Philosophy of Money* (New York: Routledge, 1990), 484.

2. David Myers, *The Pursuit of Happiness* (New York: Morrow, 1992), 150.

3. Matthew 22:37-40.

4. 1 Corinthians 13:3 (MSG).

5. Myers, 130.

6. Ephesians 2:10 (TEV).

7. Martin Seligman, *Authentic Happiness* (New York: The Free Press, 2002), 168.

8. Po Bronson, *What Should I Do with My Life?* (New York: Random House, 2002), 114.

9. Lyneka Little, "Hit List/Don McLean: The 'American Pie' Composer on His Favorite American Songwriters," Pursuits, *Wall Street Journal*, July 1, 2006, 2.

10. Erin White, "Corporate Tuition Aid Appears to Keep Workers Loyal," *Wall Street Journal*, May 21, 2007, B4.

Chapter 5: What Matters Most

1. C. S. Lewis, *The Weight of Glory and Other Addresses* (New York: Simon & Schuster, 1980), 29.

2. 2 Corinthians 5:1-5 (MSG).

3. Gerald May, quoted in John Eldredge, *The Sacred Romance* (Nashville: Nelson, 1997), 149.

4. John Eldredge, *The Sacred Romance* (Nashville: Nelson, 1997), 199.

5. Martin Seligman, *Authentic Happiness* (New York: The Free Press, 2002), 260.

6. Seligman, 14.

7. Blaise Pascal, quoted in John Eldredge, *The Journey of Desire* (Nashville: Nelson, 2000), 183.

8. Matthew 11:28.

9. 2 Corinthians 5:17.

10. John 1:12.

11. Luke 12:15 (NCV).

12. See 1 Timothy 6:17.

13. See Luke 12:16-21.

14. See Matthew 6:25-34.

15. See Proverbs 21:20.

16. See Matthew 6:24.

17. See Job 41:11; Psalm 50:12.

18. See Matthew 25:14-30.

19. Matthew 7:24-25.

20. 1 Corinthians 3:10-11.

21. 1 Corinthians 15:32.

22. See Isaiah 55:2.

23. Ecclesiastes 3:11 (TNIV).

24. Matthew 22:37.

25. Exodus 20:3.

26. Luke 15:21 (emphasis added).

27. Henri J. M. Nouwen, *The Return of the Prodigal Son* (New York: Doubleday, 1992), 42–43.

28. See 2 Peter 3:9.

29. Steve Jones, "Everything Just Fell into Place," Links Players International, http://www.linksplayers.com/steve_jones.html.

Chapter 6: Finding Joy: An "Irrational" Financial Act

1. Rich Karlgaard, "Irrational Act," *Forbes*, February 14, 2005, http://members.forbes.com/forbes/2005/0214/035.html.

2. Proverbs 3:9.

3. Matthew 6:24 (NLT).

4. Matthew 28:19-20.

5. Matthew 25:40.

6. Galatians 6:6 (NLT).

7. Malachi 3:10 (emphasis added).

8. Read about King David's attitude toward giving in 1 Chronicles 29:14-16.

9. See Genesis 1:26-27.

10. David Myers, *The Pursuit of Happiness* (New York: Morrow, 1992), 194–195.

11. Acts 20:35.

12. Matthew 6:21.

13. See Matthew 5:21-22.

14. The first example of giving 10 percent occurred well before the Law. See Genesis 14:20.

15. See Mark 12:41-43; Luke 19:1-10; 2 Corinthians 8:1-4.

16. See Deuteronomy 16:17; 1 Corinthians 16:2.

17. *Schindler's List*, DVD, directed by Steven Spielberg (1993; Universal City, CA: Universal Studios, 2004).

18. Reality of Aid 2004, "An Independent Review of Poverty Reduction and Development Assistance," http://www.realityofaid.org/roareport.php?table=roa2004&id=1 (click on "download full document").

19. Doctors Without Borders, "Field Partners: Monthly Giving Program," http://www.doctorswithoutborders.org/donate/what.cfm.

Chapter 7: Expressing Hope: An Uncommon Financial Act

1. *The Shawshank Redemption*, DVD, directed by Frank Darabont (1994; Castle Rock Entertainment, Burbank, CA: Warner Home Video, 1999).

2. Employee Benefit Research Institute, "The 2008 Retirement Confidence Survey: Americans Much More Worried About Retirement, Health Costs a Big Concern," http://ebri.org/publications/ib/index.cfm?fa=ibDisp&Content_id=3903.

3. Consumer Federation, "New Study: Typical American Household Has Net Financial Assets of $1,000," http://www.consumerfed.org/pdfs/primerica2.pdf.

4. Proverbs 13:12.

5. Bankrate.com, "Survey: Most Americans Fail the Emergency-Fund Test," http://www.bankrate.com/brm/news/sav/20060621a1.asp.

6. Emily Brandon, "Working Can Boost Your Health, Keeping You Active and Sharp," *U.S. News & World Report*, June 4, 2006, http://www.usnews.com/usnews/biztech/articles/060612/12health.htm.

7. See Matthew 6:25-34.

8. See Luke 12:16-21.

Chapter 8: Experiencing Freedom: A Brilliant Financial Act

1. Proverbs 22:7.

2. P. T. Barnum, Giga Quotes, http://www.giga-usa.com/quotes/authors/phineas_taylor_barnum_a001.htm.

3. Bankrate, Inc. calculator, http://bankrate.com/brm/calc/MinPayment.asp.

4. Psalm 37:21.

5. See Matthew 6:25-34.

6. W. H. Murray, *The Scottish Himalayan Expedition* (London: J. M. Dent & Sons Ltd., 1951), 6–7.

7. Acts 4:24.

8. Ecclesiastes 4:9-10 (NLT).

9. Bradley Dakake and Massachusetts Public Interest Research Group Consumer Team, "Deflate Your Rate: How to Lower Your Credit Card APR," http://www.masspirg.org/static/deflatereport.pdf.

10. I used the "Rapid Debt-Repayment Plan" (RDRP) calculator found on Mary Hunt's website (http://www.cheapskatemonthly.com) to determine the length of time and interest required to pay off the debts under the "fix and roll" and "accelerate the roll" scenarios. However, access to the calculator requires a paid subscription to Hunt's *Debt-Proof Living* newsletter. If I ever come across a free calculator that is as helpful, I'll post it on the "Links" page within the "Resources" tab on my website.

11. 2 Corinthians 12:7.

12. 2 Corinthians 12:8.
13. 2 Corinthians 12:9-10.

Chapter 9: Navigating with a Financial GPS

1. Financially Speaking, "Financially, Most People Flying by the Seat of Their Pants," http://www.moneypurposejoy.com/media/news_releases.
2. Thomas Stanley and William Danko, *The Millionaire Next Door* (Atlanta: Longstreet Press, 1996), 78.
3. Stanley and Danko, 41.
4. Stanley and Danko, 41.
5. Luke 12:48.

Chapter 10: Teaching Money to Dance: Part 1

1. Jonathan Clements, "Don't Blame the Latte: The Real Reason You're Not Saving More Is Closer to Home," *Wall Street Journal*, June 21, 2006, eastern edition, D1.
2. Jonathan Clements, "Retiring with a Mortgage? Here's What You Should Do," *Wall Street Journal*, September 19, 2007, eastern edition, D1.
3. *MSN* Money Staff, "Property Taxes: Where Does Your State Rank?" http://articles.moneycentral.msn.com/Taxes/Advice/PropertyTaxesWhereDoesYourStateRank.aspx.
4. Juliet Schor, *The Overspent American* (New York: Basic Books, 1998), 33.
5. Schor, 229.
6. Jonathan Welsh, "When a $38,000 Car Costs $44,000," *Wall Street Journal*, May 22, 2007, D1.
7. U.S. Department of Transportation, quoted in "Cars That Last a Million Miles," *MSN*, http://articles.moneycentral.msn.com/SavingandDebt/SaveonaCar/CarsThatLastAMillionMiles.aspx.
8. Welsh, D1.
9. Power Information Network, "Number of 'Upside-Down' Vehicle Buyers Increasing," http://www.powerinfonet.com/news/newsdetail

.asp?id=56A09C81BB884585C24C1BB884@2F38F8@138074.

10. Welsh, D3.

11. U.S. Department of Transportation, "Mean Number of Drivers, Vehicles, and Bicycles Per Household," http://www.bts.gov/ publications/highlights_of_the_2001_national_household_travel_ survey/html/table_a02.html.

12. National Association of Home Builders, "Housing Facts, Figures and Trends," May 2007, http://www.nahb.org/fileUpload_details .aspx?contentTypeID=7&contentID=2028.

Chapter 11: Teaching Money to Dance: Part 2

1. Jay MacDonald, "9 Weirdest Tax Write-offs," March 22, 2006, http://www.bankrate.com/brm/itax/news/20020201a2.asp?caret=34.

2. U.S. Department of Labor, U.S. Bureau of Labor Statistics, "Consumer Expenditures in 2005," http://www.bls.gov/cex/ csxann05.pdf.

3. Edward Fox and Stephen Hoch, "Cherry Picking," *Knowledge@ Wharton*, http://knowledge.wharton.upenn.edu/paper .cfm?paperid=1246.

4. "Historical Holiday Sales National Retail Federation," http:// www.nrf.com/modules.php?name=Pages&sp_id=696.

5. Juliet Schor, *The Overspent American* (New York: Basic Books, 1998), 80.

Chapter 12: Traveling in Financial Community

1. Parker Palmer, *Let Your Life Speak* (San Francisco: Jossey-Bass, 2000), 32.

2. See John 8:32.

3. 1 Peter 3:15.

4. John Eldredge, *The Journey of Desire* (Nashville: Nelson, 2000), 64.

5. JumpStart Coalition for Personal Financial Literacy, "Financial Literacy Still Declining Among High School Seniors, Jump$tart Coalition's 2008 Survey Shows," http://www.jumpstart.org/news .cfm.

6. See Hebrews 10:24.

7. David Myers, *The Pursuit of Happiness* (New York: Morrow, 1992), 151.

8. *The Truman Show*, DVD, directed by Peter Weir (1998; Hollywood, CA: Paramount Pictures, 1999).

Conclusion: Welcome Home

1. Luke 15:20-24.

ABOUT THE AUTHOR

M ATT BELL is a personal finance writer and speaker. His ideas have been featured in numerous publications, including the *Chicago Tribune* and *Kiplinger's Personal Finance* magazine. He has written for *ChristianityToday.com*, has served for many years in the Good $ense financial ministry, has been a guest on Crown Financial Ministry's syndicated radio program *Money Matters*, and writes two popular e-newsletters that are available free through his website, www.moneypurposejoy.com. He lives near Chicago with his wife, Jude, and their sons, Jonathan and Andrew.

WILLOW
Willow Creek Association

Vision, Training, Resources for Prevailing Churches

This resource was created to serve you and to help you build a local church that prevails. It is just one of many ministry tools published by the Willow Creek Association.

The Willow Creek Association (WCA) was created in 1992 to serve a rapidly growing number of churches from across the denominational spectrum that are committed to helping unchurched people become fully devoted followers of Christ. Membership in the WCA now numbers over 12,000 Member Churches worldwide from more than ninety denominations.

The Willow Creek Association links like-minded Christian leaders with each other and with strategic vision, training, and resources in order to help them build prevailing churches designed to reach their redemptive potential. Here are some of the ways the WCA does that.

- **The Leadership Summit** — A once-a-year, two-day conference to envision and equip Christians with leadership gifts and responsibilities. Presented live on Willow Creek's campus as well as via satellite broadcast to over 135 locations across North America — plus more than eighty international cities via videocast — this event is designed to increase the leadership effectiveness of pastors, ministry staff, volunteer church leaders, and Christians in the marketplace.

- **Ministry-Specific Conferences** — Throughout the year the WCA hosts a variety of conferences and training events — both at Willow Creek's main campus and offsite, across North America and around the world. These events are for church leaders and volunteers in areas such as small groups, children's ministry, student ministry, preaching and teaching, the arts, and stewardship.

- **Willow Creek Resources®** — Provides churches with trusted and field-tested ministry resources in such areas as leadership, volunteer ministries, spiritual formation, stewardship, evangelism, small groups, children's ministry, student ministry, the arts, and more.

- **WCA Member Benefits** — Includes substantial discounts to WCA training events, a 20 percent discount on all Willow Creek Resources®, *Defining Moments* monthly audio journal for leaders, quarterly *Willow* magazine, access to a Members-Only section on WillowNet, monthly communications and more. Member Churches also receive special discounts and premier services through the WCA's growing number of ministry partners — Select Service Providers — and save an average of $500 annually depending on the level of engagement.

For specific information about WCA conferences, resources, membership, and other ministry services contact:

Willow Creek Association
P.O. Box 3188
Barrington, IL 60011-3188
Phone: 847.570.9812
Fax: 847.765.5046
www.willowcreek.com

Freed-Up Financial Living: How to Get There with Biblical Principles

Dick Towner, John Tofilon, Shannon Plate

Freed-Up Financial Living combines encouraging, grace-filled teaching with biblical principles and practical application tools that will transform your heart as well as your finances. In six, one-hour sessions you'll discover biblical foundations and practical tools to help you develop a personalized financial plan and achieve your financial goals. Designed for use by small groups, the material can also be adapted for use by individuals or larger groups in a seminar setting.

DVD UPC 633277007436
Participant's Workbook ISBN 074419637X

Freed-Up Financial Living Ministry Leader's Kit

The *Freed-Up Financial Living Ministry Leader's Kit* includes everything you need to launch and lead a year-round stewardship ministry in your church:

- Quick-Start Guide
- The *Freed Up Financial Living* DVD with complete course teaching for six, one-hour sessions
- Three Participant's Workbooks
- Teaching notes and tools (downloadable)
- Promotional materials (downloadable)
- The book *Money, Purpose, Joy* by Matt Bell

Complete Kit ISBN 074419623X

Order your copies today at www.willowcreek.com/resources

Money, Purpose, Joy – Don't Forget the Discussion Guide for Small Groups and a Personal Workbook!

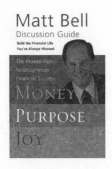

Money, Purpose, Joy: Discussion Guide
Matt Bell
978-1-60006-322-0

This discussion guide will stimulate meaningful interaction among couples, small groups, Bible studies, and Christian growth classes as well as encourage each participant's individual understanding and application of the life-changing principles found in *Money, Purpose, Joy*.

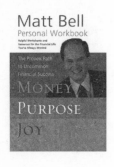

Money, Purpose, Joy: Personal Workbook
978-1-60006-321-3

Worksheets, forms, and additional resources to help you achieve the financial life you've always wanted.